Valerius Terminus: of the Interpretation of Nature

by

Sir Francis Bacon

The Echo Library 2007

Published by

The Echo Library

Echo Library
131 High St.
Teddington
Middlesex TW11 8HH

www.echo-library.com

Please report serious faults in the text to complaints@echo-library.com

ISBN 978-1-40682-383-7

PREFACE

THE following fragments of a great work on the Interpretation of Nature were first published in Stephens's Letters and Remains [1734]. They consist partly of detached passages, and partly of an epitome of twelve chapters of the first book of the proposed work. The detached passages contain the first, sixth, and eighth chapters, and portions of the fourth, fifth, seventh, ninth, tenth, eleventh, and sixteenth. The epitome contains an account of the contents of all the chapters from the twelfth to the twenty-sixth inclusive, omitting the twentieth, twentythird, and twenty-fourth. Thus the sixteenth chapter is mentioned both in the epitome and among the detached passages, and we are thus enabled to see that the two portions of the following tract belong to the same work, as it appears from both that the sixteenth chapter was to treat of the doctrine of idola.

It is impossible to ascertain the motive which determined Bacon to give to the supposed author the name of Valerius Terminus, or to his commentator, of whose annotations we have no remains, that of Hermes Stella. It may be conjectured that by the name Terminus he intended to intimate that the new philosophy would put an end to the wandering of mankind in search of truth, that it would be the TERMINUS AD QUEM in which when it was once attained the mind would finally acquiesce.

Again, the obscurity of the text was to be in some measure removed by the annotations of Stella; not however wholly, for Bacon in the epitome of the eighteenth chapter commends the manner of publishing knowledge "whereby it shall not be to the capacity nor taste of all, but shall as it were single and adopt his reader." Stella was therefore to throw a kind of starlight on the subject, enough to prevent the student's losing his way, but not much more.

However this may be, the tract is undoubtedly obscure, partly from the style in which it is written, and partly from its being only a fragment. It is at the same time full of interest, inasmuch as it is the earliest type of the INSTAURATIO...

Note to Preface by James Spedding:
The manuscript from which Robert Stephens printed these fragments was found among some loose papers placed in his hands by the Earl of Oxford, and is now in the British Museum; Harl. manuscripts 6462. It is a thin paper volume of the quarto size, written in the hand of one of Bacon's servants, with corrections, erasures, and interlineations in his own.

The chapters of which it consists are both imperfect in themselves (all but three),—some breaking off abruptly, others being little more than tables of contents,—and imperfect in their connexion with each other; so much so as to suggest the idea of a number of separate papers loosely put together. But it was not so (and the fact is important) that the volume itself was actually made up. However they came together, they are here fairly and consecutively copied out. Though it be a collection of fragments therefore, it is such a collection as Bacon thought worthy not only of being preserved, but of being transcribed into a volume; and a particular account of it will not be out of place.

The contents of the manuscript before Bacon touched it may be thus described.

1. A titlepage, on which is written "VALERIUS TERMINUS of the Interpretation of Nature, with the annotations of HERMES STELLA."

2. "Chapter I.   Of the limits and end of knowledge;" with a running title, "Of the Interpretation of Nature."

3. "The chapter immediately following the Inventory; being the 11th in order."

4. "A part of the 9th chapter, immediately precedent to the Inventory, and inducing the same."

5. "The Inventory, or an enumeration and view of inventions already discovered and in use, together with a note of the wants and the nature of the supplies; being the 10th chapter, and this a fragment only of the same."

6. Part of a chapter, not numbered, "Of the internal and profound errors and superstitions in the nature of the mind, and of the four sorts of Idols or fictions which offer themselves to the understanding in the inquisition of knowledge."

7. "Of the impediments of knowledge; being the third chapter, the preface only of it."

8. "Of the impediments which have been in the times and in diversion of wits; being the fourth chapter."

9. "Of the impediments of knowledge for want of a true succession of wits, and that hitherto the length of one man's life hath been the greatest measure of knowledge; being the fifth chapter."

10. "That the pretended succession of wits hath been evil placed, forasmuch as after variety of sects and opinions the most popular and not the truest prevaileth and weareth out the rest; being the sixth chapter."

11. "Of the impediments of knowledge in handling it by parts, and in slipping off particular sciences from the root and stock of universal knowledge; being the seventh chapter."

12. "That the end and scope of knowledge hath been generally mistaken, and that men were never well advised what it was they sought" (part of a chapter not numbered).

13. "An abridgment of divers chapters of the first book;" namely, the 12th, 13th, and 14th, (over which is a running title "Of active knowledge;") and (without any running title) the 15th, 16th, 17th, 18th], 19th, 21st, 22nd, 25th, and 26th. These abridgments have no headings; and at the end is written, "The end of the Abridgment of the first book of the Interpretation of Nature."

Such was the arrangement of the manuscript as the transcriber left it; which I have thought worth preserving, because I seem to see traces in it of two separate stages in the developement of the work; the order of the chapters as they are transcribed being probably the same in which Bacon wrote them; and the numbers inserted at the end of the headings indicating the order in which, when he placed them in the transcriber's hands, it was his intention to arrange them; and because it proves at any rate that at that time the design of the whole book was clearly laid out in his mind.

There is nothing, unfortunately, to fix the DATE of the transcript, unless it be implied in certain astronomical or astrological symbols written on the blank outside of the volume; in which the figures 1603 occur. This may possibly be the transcriber's note of the time when he finished his work; for which (but for one circumstance which I shall mention presently) I should think the year 1603 is likely a date as any; for we know from a letter of Bacon's, dated 3rd July 1603, that he had at that time resolved "to meddle as little as possible in the King's causes," and to "put his ambition wholly upon his pen;" and we know from the ADVANCEMENT OF LEARNING that in 1605 he was engaged upon a work entitled "The Interpretation of Nature:" to which I may add that there is in the Lambeth Library a copy of a letter from Bacon to Lord Kinlosse, dated 25th March, 1603, and written in the same hand as this manuscript.

Bacon's corrections, if I may judge from the character of the handwriting, were inserted a little later; for it is a fact that about the beginning of James's reign his writing underwent a remarkable change, from the hurried Saxon hand full of large sweeping curves and with letters imperfectly formed and connected, which he wrote in Elizabeth's time, to a small, neat, light, and compact one, formed more upon the Italian model which was then coming into fashion; and when these corrections were made it is evident that this new character had become natural to him and easy. It is of course impossible to fix the precise date of such a change,—the more so because his autographs of this period are very scarce,—but whenever it was that he corrected this manuscript, it is evident that he then considered it worthy of careful revision. He has not merely inserted a sentence here and there, altered the numbers of the chapters, and added words to the headings in order to make the description more exact; but he has taken the trouble to add the running title wherever it was wanting, thus writing the words "of the Interpretation of Nature" at full lengths not less than eighteen times over; and upon the blank space of the titlepage he has written out a complete table of contents. In short, if he had been preparing the manuscript for the press or for a fresh transcript, he could not have done it more completely or carefully,—only that he has given no directions for altering the order of the chapters so as to make it correspond with the numbers. And hence I infer that up to the time when he made these corrections, this was the form of the great work on which he was engaged: it was a work concerning the Interpretation of Nature; which was to begin where the NOVUM ORGANUM begins; and of which the first book was to include all the preliminary considerations preparatory to the exposition of the formula.

I place this fragment here in deference to Mr. Ellis's decided opinion that it was written before the ADVANCEMENT OF LEARNING. The positive ground indeed which he alleges in support of that conclusion I am obliged to set aside, as founded, I think, upon a misapprehension; and the supposition that no part of it was written later involves a difficulty which I cannot yet get over to my own satisfaction. But that the body of it was written earlier I see no reason to doubt; and if so, this is its proper place.

The particular point on which I venture to disagree with Mr. Ellis I have stated in a note upon his preface to the NOVUM ORGANUM, promising at the same time a fuller explanation of the grounds of my own conclusion, which I will now give.

The question is, whether the "Inventory" in the 10th chapter of VALERIUS TERMINUS was to have exhibited a general survey of the state of knowledge corresponding with that which fills the second book of the ADVANCEMENT OF LEARNING. I think not.

It is true indeed that the title of that 10th chapter,—namely, "The Inventory, or an enumeration and view of inventions already discovered and in use, with a note of the wants and the nature of the supplies",—has at first sight a considerable resemblance to the description of the contents of the second book of the ADVANCEMENT OF LEARNING,—namely, "A general and faithful perambulation of learning, with an inquiry what parts thereof lie fresh and waste, and not improved and converted by the industry of Man;... wherein nevertheless my purpose is at this time to note only omissions and deficiencies, and not to make any redargutions of errors," and so on. But an "enumeration of INVENTIONS" is not the same thing as "a perambulation of LEARNING;" and it will be found upon closer examination that the "Inventory" spoken of in VALERIUS TERMINUS does really correspond to one, and one only, of the fiftyone Desiderata set down at the end of the DE AUGMENTIS; viz. that INVENTARIUM OPUM HUMANARUM, which was to be an appendix to the MAGIA NATURALIS. See DE AUG. iii. 5. This will appear clearly by comparing the descriptions of the two.

In the ADVANCEMENT OF LEARNING Bacon tells us that there are two points of much purpose pertaining to the department of Natural Magic: the first of which is, "That there be made a calendar resembling an Inventory of the ESTATE OF MAN, containing ALL THE INVENTIONS, BEING THE WORKS OR FRUITS OF NATURE OR ART, which are now extant AND OF WHICH MAN IS ALREADY POSSESSED; out of which doth naturally result a note what things are yet held impossible or not invented; which calendar will be the more artificial and serviceable if to every reputed impossibility you add what thing is extant which cometh the nearest in degree to that impossibility: to the end that by these optatives and essentials man's inquiry may be the more awake in deducing direction of works from the speculation of causes."

The Inventory which was to have been inserted in the 10th chapter of VALERIUS TERMINUS is thus introduced:—"The plainest method and most directly pertinent to this intention will be to make distribution of SCIENCES, ARTS, INVENTIONS, WORKS, and their portions, ACCORDING TO THE USE AND TRIBUTE WHICH THEY YIELD AND RENDER TO THE

CONDITION OF MAN'S LIFE; and under those several uses, being as several offices of provisions, to charge and tax what may be reasonably exacted or demanded,... and then upon those charges and taxations to distinguish and present as it were in several columns what is extant and already found, and what is DEFECTIVE AND FURTHER TO BE PROVIDED. Of which provisions because in many of them, after the manner of slothful and faulty accomptants, it will be returned by way of excuse that no such are to be had, it will be fit to give some light OF THE NATURE OF THE SUPPLIES; whereby it will evidently appear that they are to be compassed and procured." And that the calendar was to deal, not with knowledge in general, but only with arts and sciences of invention in its more restricted sense—the PARS OPERATIVA DE NATURA (DE AUG. iii. 5.)—appears no less clearly from the opening of the 11th chapter, which was designed immediately to follow the "Inventory." "It appeareth then what is now in proposition, not by general circumlocution but by particular note. No former philosophy," etc. etc. "but the revealing and discovering of NEW INVENTIONS AND OPERATIONS,... the nature and kinds of which inventions HAVE BEEN DESCRIBED as they could be discovered," etc. If further evidence were required of the exact resemblance between the Inventory of VALERIUS TERMINUS and the Inventarium of the ADVANCEMENT and the DE AUGMENTIS, I might quote the end of the 9th chapter, where the particular expressions correspond, if possible, more closely still. But I presume that the passages which I have given are enough; and that the opinion which I have elsewhere expressed as to the origin of the ADVANCEMENT OF LEARNING,—namely, that the writing of it was a by-thought and no part of the work on the Interpretation of Nature as originally designed,—will not be considered inconsistent with the evidence afforded by these fragments.

That the VALERIUS TERMINUS was composed before the ADVANCEMENT, though a conclusion not deducible from the Inventory, is nevertheless probable: but to suppose that it was so composed EXACTLY IN ITS PRESENT FORM, involves, as I said, a difficulty; which I will now state. The point is interesting, as bearing directly upon the developement in Bacon's mind of the doctrine of Idols; concerning which see preface to NOVUM ORGANUM, note C. But I have to deal with it here merely as bearing upon the probable date of this fragment.

In treating of the department of Logic in the ADVANCEMENT, Bacon notices as altogether wanting "the particular elenches or cautions against three false appearances" or fallacies by which the mind of man is beset: the "caution" of which, he says, "doth extremely import the true conduct of human judgment." These false appearances he describes, though he does not give their names; and they correspond respectively to what he afterwards called the Idols of the Tribe, the Cave, and the Forum. But he makes no mention of the fourth; namely, the Idols of the Theatre. Now in VALERIUS TERMINUS we find two separate passages in which the Idols are mentioned; and in both all four are enumerated, and all by name; though what he afterwards called Idols of the Forum, he there calls Idols of the Palace; and it seems to me very unlikely that, if when he wrote the ADVANCEMENT he had already formed that classification he should have omitted all mention of the Idols of the Theatre; for though it is true that that was not the place to discuss them, and therefore in the corresponding passage of the DE AUGMENTIS they are noticed as to be passed by "for the present," yet they are noticed by name, and in all Bacon's later writings the confutation of them holds a very prominent place.

To me the most probable explanation of the fact is this. I have already shown that between the composition and the transcription of these fragments the design of the work appears to have undergone a considerable change; the order of the chapters being entirely altered. We have only to suppose therefore that they were composed before the ADVANCEMENT and transcribed after, and that in preparing them for the transcriber Bacon made the same kind of alterations in the originals which he afterwards made upon the transcript, and the difficulty disappears. Nothing would be easier than to correct "three" into "four," and insert "the Idols of the Theatre" at the end of the sentence.

And this reminds me (since I shall have so much to do with these questions of date) to suggest a general caution with regard to them all; namely, that in the case of fragments like these, the comparison of isolated passages can hardly ever be relied upon for evidence of the date or order of composition, or of the progressive developement of the writer's views; and for this simple reason,—we can never be sure that the passages as they now stand formed part of the original writing. The copy of the fragment which we have may be (as there is reason to believe this was) a transcript from several loose papers, written at different periods and containing alterations or additions made from time to time. We may know perhaps that when Bacon published the ADVANCEMCNT OF LEARNING he was ignorant of some fact with which he afterwards became acquainted; we may find in one of these fragments,—say the TEMPORIS PARTUS MASCULUS,—a passage implying acquaintance with that fact. Does it follow that the TEMPORIS PARTUS MASCULUS was written after the ADVANCEMENT OF LEARNING? No; for in looking over the manuscript long after it was written, he may have observed and corrected the error. And we cannot conclude that he at the same time altered the whole composition so as to bring it into accordance with the views he then held; for that might be too long a work. He may have inserted a particular correction, but meant to rewrite the whole; and if so, in spite of the later date indicated by that particular passage, the body of the work would still represent a stage in his opinions anterior to the ADVANCEMENT OF LEARNING.

I have felt some doubt whether in printing this fragment, I should follow the example of Stephens, who gave it exactly as he found it; or that of later editors, who have altered the order of the chapters so as to make it agree with the numbers. The latter plan will perhaps, upon the whole, be the more convenient. There can he little doubt that the numbers of the chapters indicate the order in which Bacon meant them to be read; and if any one wishes to compare it with the order in which they seem to have been written, he has only to look at Bacon's table of contents, which was made with reference to the transcript, and which I give unaltered, except as to the spelling.

of the Interpretation of Nature with the Annotations of a few fragments of the first book, viz.

1. The first chapter entire. {Of the ends and limits of knowledge.}
2. A portion of the 11th chapter. {Of the scale.}
3. A small portion of the 9th chapter {being an Inducement to the Inventory.}
4. A small portion of the 10th chapter {being the preface to the Inventory.}
5. A small portion of the 16th chapter {being a preface to the inward elenches of the mind.}
6. A small portion of the 4th chapter. {Of the impediments of knowledge in general.}
7. A small portion of the 5th chapter. {Of the diversion of wits.}
8. The 6th chapter entire. {Of}
9. A portion of the 7th chapter.
10. The 8th chapter entire.
11. Another portion of the 9th chapter.
12. The Abridgment of the 12. 13. 14. 15. 16. 17. 18. 19. 21. 22. 25. 26th chapters of the first book.
13. The first chapter of {the} a book of the same argument written in Latin and destined {for} to be {traditionary} separate and not public.

None of the Annotations of Stella are set down in these fragments.

[The title] is written in the transcriber's hand: all that follows in Bacon's. The words between brackets have a line drawn through them. For an exact facsimile of the whole [see Contents pages 1 and 2].

[13.] refers to the first chapter of the TEMPORIS PARTUS MASCULUS; which follows in the manuscript volume, but not here. It is important as bearing upon the date of that fragment.

Valerius Terminus: Of The Interpretation Of Nature

THE first chapter of VALERIUS TERMINUS by Francis Bacon

An annotated version compiled and edited by Dr. Gisela Engel (Johann Wolfgang Goethe-Universitaet Frankfurt am Main with the assistance of Dr. Harvey Wheeler (Ret. USC, Martha Boas Distinguished Research Professor at USC) and aided by Melek Hasgün, Simone Wirthmann, Antje Peters, Martina Glebocki, Carsten Jägler, Katja Morawek, Cora Hartmann (students at Johann Wolfgang Goethe-Universitaet Frankfurt am Main).

Orignal Text

Valerius Terminus: Of the Interpretation{1} of Nature

Annotations

1A.

The word "interpretation" occurs also e.g. in the title of the essay DE INTERPRETATIONE NATURAE PROEMIUM (1603; in Spedding vol. III) and in his definition of man as "the servant and interpreter of Nature" (IV,47). This definition of man is the same definition that we find in the magico-alchemical tradition which is in general refuted by Bacon. Paolo Rossi ("Bacon's idea of science", in: THE CAMBRIDGE COMPANION TO BACON, ed. by Markku Peltonen [1996], 25-46) gives the following comment:

"Bacon condemned magic and alchemy on ethical grounds. He accused them of imposture and of megalomania. He refuted their non-participatory method and their intentional unintelligibility, their attempt to replace human sweat by a few drops of elixir. But he borrows from the magico-alchemical tradition the idea that man can attempt to make himself the master of nature. Bacon understands knowledge not as contemplation or recognition, but as VENATIO, a hunt, an exploration of unknown lands, a discovery of the unknown. Nature can be transformed from its foundations. Bacon's definition of man as "the servant and interpreter of Nature" is the same definition we find in the magico alchemical tradition, for instance in the texts of Cornelius Agrippa von Nettesheim.

But for all the exponents of magic and alchemistic culture, the texts of ancient wisdom take the form of sacred texts which indude secrets that only a few men can decipher The truth is hidden in the past and in the profound. Like when dealing with sacred texts, it is necessary continuously to go BEYOND THE LETTER, in search of a message which is more and more hidden.The secret message expresses a Truth which is at the Origins and which is always the same.

In the Hermetic tradition, as in the tradition of Platonism, the natural world is conceived as the image or living manifestation of God. Understanding nature can reveal the presence in the world of divine ideas and archetypes. Bacon's rejection of any natural philosophy founded on allegorical interpretations of Scriptures meant a withdrawal from exemplarism and symbolism, both common features of mediaeval philosophy and still flourishing in the seventeenth century. As all works —says Bacon— show the power and ability of their maker, but not his image, so God's works "do shew the omnipotency and wisdom of the maker but not his image" (III, 350). The distinction between the will and power of God, so fully and subtly present in Baconian texts, is very important. "The heavens declare the glory of God, and the firmament showeth his handworks": this verse from the Psalms (18,2) is quoted by Bacon several times. The image of the world, immediately after the Word, is a sign of the divine wisdom and power, and yet the Scriptures do not call the world ,"the image of God," but regard it only as "the work of his hands," neither do they speak of any image of God other than man. Theology is concerned with knowing the book of the word of God, natural philosophy studies the book of God's works. The book of Scripture reveals the will of God, the book of nature, his power. The study of nature has nothing to say about God's essence or his will (IV; 340-3).

Bacon proposed to the European culture an alternative view of science. For him science had a public, democratic, and collaborative character, individual efforts contributing to its general success. In science, as Bacon conceives it, truly effective results (not the illusory achievements of magicians and alchemists) can be attained only through collaboration among researchers, circulation of results, and clarity of language. Scientific understanding is not an individual undertaking. The extension of man's power over nature is never the work of a single investigator who keeps his results secret, but is the fruit of an organized community financed by the state or by public bodies. Every reform of learning is always a reform also of cultural institutions and universities.

Not only a new image of science, but also a new portrait of the "natural philosopher" took shape in Bacon's writings. This portrait differed both from that of the ancient philosopher or sage and from the image of the saint, the monk, the university professor, the courtier, the perfect prince, the magus. The values and the ends theorized for the composite groups of intellectuals and artisans who contributed in the early seventeenth century to the development of science were different from the goals of individual sanctity or literary immortality and from the aims of an exceptional and "demonic" personality.

A chaste patience, a natural modesty, grave and composed manners, a smiling pity are the characteristics of the man of science in Bacon's portrait of him. In the REDARGUTIO PHILOSOPHIARUM Bacon wrote:

Then he told me that in Paris a friend had taken him along and introduced him to a gathering, 'the sight of which', he said, 'would rejoice your eyes. It was the happiest experience of my life'. There were some fifty men there, all of mature years, not a young man among them, all bearing the stamp of dignity and probity... At his entry they were chatting easily among themselves but sitting in rows as if expecting somebody. Not long after there entered to them a man of peaceful and serene air, save that his face had become habituated to the expression of pity... he took his seat, not on a platform or pulpit, but on level with the rest and delivered the following address. (III, 559; Farrington's translation).

Bacon's portrait doubtless resembles Galileo or Einstein more than it does the turbulent Paracelsus or the unquiet and skittish Cornelius Agrippa. The titanic bearing of the Renaissance magus is now supplanted by a classical composure similar to that of the "conversations" of the earliest Humanists. Also in Galileo's

DIALOGO and in Descartes's RECHERCHE DE LA VERITÉ we find the same familiar tone and style of conversation in which [Descartes wrote] "several friends, frankly and without ceremony, disclose the best of their thoughts to each other." But there is besides, in Bacon, the quiet confidence that comes from knowing the new powers made available to man by technology and collaboration. The new kind of learning, for which Bacon is searching, must get away from touches of genius, arbitrary conclusions, chance, hasty summaries. The emphasis laid by Bacon on the social factor in scientific research and in determining its ends, places his philosophy on a radically different plane from that of the followers of Hermetic tradition."

In DE SAPIENTIA VETERUM Bacon describes Orpheus as the mythical prototype of the philosopher ("Orpheus sive Philosophia", VI, 646-649).

1B.

Bacon gives the following definition of "interpretation: "that reason which is elicited from facts by a just and methodological process, I call INTERPRETATION OF NATURE" (IV, 51). Now, this definition means a harsh critique of Aristotelianism, Scholasticism and Ramism. Michel Malherbe comments on this:

"The main and most characteristic feature of Bacon's epistemology is that it rests upon a single method, which is INDUCTION... It must help the understanding on its way toward truth... Thus, true knowledge will go from a lower certainty to a higher liberty and from a lower liberty to a higher certainty, and so on. This rule is the basic principle of Bacon's theory of science; prepared in the natural and experimental history, determining the relationship between the tables of presence, it governs the induction of axioms and the abstraction of notions and ordains the divisions of sciences within the general system of knowledge. It is well known that this rule of invention originates in Ramus's methodology and, more formerly, in Aristotle's POSTERIOR ANALYTICS. To characterize the nature of the premises required for the foundation of true demonstrations, Aristotle had set down three criteria: the predicate must be true in every instance of its subject; it must be part of the essential nature of the subject; and it must be universal, that is, related to the subject by itself and QUA itself. Aristotle was defining first propositions as being essential propositions; and he referred universality to necessity and extension to comprehension These three criteria were much commented upon during the whole scholastic period, and were transformed, or rather extended, by Ramus and others in the sixteenth century. Whereas in Aristotle they had expressed the initial conditions of any conclusive syllogism, in Ramus they became the conditions of every systematic art: within a system, methodically organized for the exhibiting of knowledge, any statement must be taken in its full extension, it must join things which are necessarily related and it must be equivalent to a definition. But these rules for syllogistic or dialectic art in Aristotle or Ramus become rules for inductive invention in Bacon: and their meaning is quite different. With the rule of certainty and liberty, Bacon aims at directiy opposing the old logic, infected by syllogistic or rhetoric formalism.

By its title, the NOVUM ORGANUM makes Bacon's ambition clear: to replace the Aristotelian organon, which has governed all knowledge until the end of the sixteenth century with an entirely new logical instrument, a new method for the progress and profit of human science. And the Chancellor proclaims that he has achieved his aim, if posterity acknowledges that, even if he has failed to discover new truths or produce new works, he will have built the means to discover such truths or to produce such works (III, 520). He insists that his method has nothing to do with the old one nor does it try to improve it. And he puts out the choice in these terms:

There are and can be only two ways of searching into and discovering truth. The one flies from the senses and particulars to the most general axioms, and from these principles, the truth of which it takes tor settled and immoveable, proceeds to judgment and to the discovery of middle axioms. And this way is now in fashion. The other derives axioms from the senses and particulars, rising by a gradual and unbroken ascent, so that it arrives at the most general axioms last of all. This is the true way, but as yet untried. (IV, 50)

When it is left to itself, the understanding follows the first way, hastily applies itself to reality and generates ANTICIPATIONS OF NATURE. But "that reason which is elicited from facts by a just and methodological process, I call

INTERPRETATION OF NATURE"
(IV, 51).

Taken as a whole, Bacon's critique comes to this: from a formal point of view, Aristotle's syllogism is essentially a logic for deductive reasoning, which goes from the principles to the consequences, from the premises to the conclusions. And, of course, in this kind of reasoning, the truth of the conclusions is necessarily derived from the truth of the premises, so that knowledge will start with primary truths that are supposed to be necessary and universal, that is, essential. Now, Bacon asks, how does the mind acquire the knowledge of these primary truths, since, as it is allowed by Aristotle himself, all knowledge starts with experience, which experience is always contingent and particular? How does the mind go from the empirical knowledge of facts or sensible effects (phenomena) to the knowledge of the very nature of things? The formal necessity of the syllogism (or deductive reasoning) makes the old logic forget the prejudicial question of how we set up first principles. Therefore, any attempt to define the valid form of theories must go through the inquiry upon how we establish truth.

From this general critique, it is easy to understand Bacon's various comments on the old organon. First, since such a logic induces a kind of double start, the empirical one and the rational one, and since it confuses the origin of knowledge with its foundation, the mind is condemned to jump immediately from empirical particulars to first principles (or axioms, in Bacon's terms) and to render superfluous the required induction which would gradually lead from one point to the other. This instantaneous slip from empirical data to rational and essential dogmas is made possible by the very nature of the human mind. Left to itself, the mind hurries toward certainty; it is prone to gain assent and consent; it fills the imagination with idols, untested generalities. And it is this natural haste and prejudice which gives mental activity its anticipative form. By themselves, anticipations draw the most general principles from immediate experience, in order to proceed, as quickly as possible, to the formal deduction of consequences. Therefore, however paradoxical it may appear, the old logic is unduly empirical and unduly logical. And the critique of formalism [formalism draws the conclusions from the premises without inquiring upon the truth of the premises] must be attended by the critique of the nature of the human mind.

The human mind is so disposed that it relies on the senses, which provide it with the rudiments of all knowledge. Of course, Bacon argues, we cannot get any information about things except with the senses, and skeptics are wrong when, questioning them, they plunge the mind into despair. "But by far the greatest hindrance and aberration of the human understanding proceeds from the dulness, incompetency, and deceptions of the senses" (IV, 58). On the one hand, they are too dull and too gross, and let the more subtle parts of nature escape our observation: their range is limited to the most conspicuous information. On the other hand, they are misleading, by a fundamental illusion: they offer things to the mind according to the measure of human nature. "For it is a false assertion that the sense of man is the measure of things. On the contrary, all perceptions as well of the sense as of the mind are according to the measure of the individual and not according to the measure of the universe" (IV, 54). In order to have access to reality, we have to rectify their information and reduce a double delusion: the illusion that the sensible qualities offered by them are the real determinations of things and the illusion that things are divided according to our human sensibility (IV, 194 et sq.).

Thus we can understand a third critique against the old method: the Aristotelian logic rests upon a metaphysics which believes that sensible experience gives the human mind the things as they are, with their essential qualities, and that philosophy can be satisfied with taking empirical phenomena for the true reality of nature, thanks to a mere generalization that erases the particular circumstances of existence. Nevertheless, empirically qualified existences are not to be mistaken for the things themselves. So far, Bacon is undoubtedly a modern, since he claims that the object of knowledge is reality and that reality, if it can be inductively known from empirical data, cannot be reduced to the matter of experience.

Bacon's fourth censure of the old logic follows from this. He agrees with the sixteenth-century dialecticians that Aristotle was wrong when he thought that understanding could skip, without the hard work of induction, from what is immediately given to the senses to what is posed in the first principles of science. Aristotle wanted to know the truth, but did not explain the method of invention. On the other hand, the dialecticians, giving up the attempt to set up the first principles (and thereby the traditional Aristotelian demonstrative science), gave up any attempt to reach the truth. They only retained the deductive and systematic form of discourse to introduce order into men's opinions, and maintained that invention could be reduced to the mere search for arguments, that is, for probable reasons invented to persuade or convince.

Bacon, however, wants to promote the idea of an inductive science and argues that Aristotle's mistake affects the syllogistic form. In the fourth chapter of the fifth book of the DE AUGMENTIS, Bacon develops a remarkable critique of the syllogism and is partly responsible for the widespread disregard of formal logic in the seventeenth and eighteenth centuries.

According to Bacon, "in all inductions, whether in good or vicious form the same action of the mind which inventeth, judgeth" (III, 392). One cannot find without proving, nor prove without finding. But this is not the case in the syllogism: "for the proof being not immediate but by mean, the invention of the mean is one thing, and the judgement of the consequence is another, the one exciting only, the other examining" (III, 392). The syllogism needs the means (the middle term) so that the derived conclusion amounts to a proof. But since the syllogism is incapable of inventing the middle term, it must have been known before. In other words, syllogistic form leaves the invention of the middle term to the natural shrewdness of the mind or to good fortune. Thus, it is because of its own demonstrative form that the syllogism is unable to provide a method of truth and is useless for science.

By now it is clear why the old logic and the knowledge which is built on it are unable to produce works or why the extant works "are due to chance and experience rather than to sciences" (IV, 48). To deduce practical effects, the mind must know real causes or laws of nature. Since the old method does not supply the mind with the means of inventing causes and does not set up the scale of the intermediate propositions that are needed to reduce sensible experience and reach the real science, or to derive rightly and by degrees the consequences from the principles, it is not surprising that invented works are too few and not very useful for men's lives. Thus, from the start in sensible experience to the end in practical deduction, this old method is of no use. And an entirely new one must be proposed, which will be able to carry the human mind from empirical data to the real causes, to supply it with the means of invention, to justify the position of first truths and to manage a secure deduction of practical consequences. And, as the critique of the old logic has to be understood as a whole, so the interpretation of nature has to be conceived as a continuous attempt, proceeding by degrees, by successive stages, to invent truth and to derive works. ("Bacon's method of science", in: THE CAMBRIDGE COMPANION TO BACON. ed. by Markku Peltonen [1996], 76-82).
1C.

Harvey Wheeler comments:

Most historians of the philosophy of science are unfamiliar with Bacon's transformation of his innovative theory of juridical lawfinding into scientific empiricist lawfinding. Baconian law-finding is not to be confused with cause-finding in modern "classical" physics.

Bacon's quest changed as he matured. In VALERIUS TERMINUS he is writing in English, trying to lay the groundwork for the validity of the co-existence of Religion and Science.

Bacon's early experimental treatises— like Dense and Rare—are experimental and of limited value. Historians of the philosophy of science have little trouble in disposing these early experimentalist efforts of Bacon.

His work on sound was somewhat better—experimental-theoretical. It is a post-pythagorean theory of harmonics and still not appropriately analyzed. Contemproary musicologists like to quote the passages on sound in NEW ATLANTIS for being compatible with today's approach to music.

By the time of the Novum Organum Bacon was seeking a more "general theory of science." Its 'logic machine' (Hooke) was designed to be relevant to all non-theological domains.

However, most Bacon interpreters evaluate his science in contrast to the prior Aristotelian approaches and in comparison to the Ramist approaches of Bacon's day. He rejected them both.

Scholars then look beyond Bacon and evaluate his logic machine in contrast to the "classical mechanics" of Newtonian Optics (physics): linear time-sequence prediction.

Bacon was not seeking that type of "cause/prediction"science. He was seeking hidden, "unwritten" "laws" of nature, more on the model of Pasteur than of Newton.

Any treatment that tries to interpret Bacon's Logic Machine in the light of what classical physics called "science" will distort Bacon's meaning and achievement.

Note: if a scholar's interpretation of Bacon's Science does not square with the detailed description of the application of Bacon's science in "Salomon's House" in NEW ATLANTIS, it should be viewed with scepticism.

Bacon's science is more applicable to what we call post-modern neo-hermeutics than to Newtonian mechanics. (Patrick Heelan is good on post-modern neo-hermeneutics.)

Consider: why did Bacon conclude that his New Logic Machine would produce scientific knowledge in the form of aphorisms and apothegms— not linear time-sequence predictions?

To summarize the above:: Most contemporary interpreters of Bacon evaluate his science by comparison with Newtonian mechanics. If one interprets Bacon on the basis of classical mechanics, the result will not truly reflect Bacon's science.

A more fruitful modern model is the Watson-Crick type of "science" illustrated by their discovery of the double helix. Their process, as described carefully in Watson's book, could have been lifted from Bacon. It was not. But the point is that it tells of a highly successful, highly empiricist (in Bacon's and Kant's meaning of phenomenological empiricism) approach to the "understanding" of the "unwritten laws" of cell theory and genetics.

NOTE: It is very instructive to study why Linus Pauling failed to dsiscover the genetic code. He was an expert in the physics of biochemistry and applied quantum theory to molecular biology. His theory of the molecular bond won a Nobel Laureate.

Read Watson's explanation of why Pauling failed to crack the genetic code.

Guenther Stent, the molecular biologist of U.C. Berkeley is an avowed Kantian who narrowly missed cracking the genetic code, His philosophy of science is highly relevant to the application of neo-hermeneutics to contemporary biology.

Today's philosophy of physics, as developed by John Wheeler and David Bohm describes a "Baconian" idea of the "participant-observer universe" to account "scientifically" and empirically for the evidence produced in post-modern physics.

I hold to two points that may not persuade others. The first is the relevance of "law-finding" to the phenemonological empiricism at the heart of Bacon's Nov Org logic machine—as contrasted with his early experimentalism. The second is the standard for us to use in evaluating Bacon's science. Those who apply the model of science widespread in the social sciences and humanities during the 19th and mid 20th centuries—essentially a model based upon pre-Einsteinian physics—argue that Bacon's science is not "science."

In the last half of the 20th century "science" in both the "hard" and "soft" sciences underwent the so-called "second scientific revolution." The results, in physics and biology, produced a phenomenology and an empiricism that were both quite compatible with the pre-Newtonian science of Bacon.

About 80% of the actual research in laboratories done today by scientists of all fields, (unaware) follows remarkably closely to the process explained by Bacon in Novum Organum and described in New Atlantis—except that taskforce research is not today quite as well organized as was described by Bacon in New Atlantis.

In thinking of Bacon's philosophy of science remember the three features in the Latin of Novum Organum: Schematismus, Processus, Form. These operations, which have counterparts in the "case method" of searching for the implicit unwritten law behind a series of judge rulings, cannot be understood from a reading of the Ellis translation. Nobody who works from that version can understand, nor do justice to, Bacon's science.

with the Annotations of Hermes Stella{2} Harley MSS.6463

2. Franz Trägfer sums up the discussion on "Hermes Stella" and "Valerius Terminus" "Der Titel des Fragments wurde zweimal entscheidend interpretiert. Ellis (Vorwort, 201/2):

"It is impossible to ascertain the motive which determined Bacon to give the supposed author the name of Valerius Terminus, or to his commentator, of whose annotations we have no remains, that of Hermes Stella. It may be conjectured that by the name Terminus he intended to intimate that the new philosophy would put an end to the wandering of mankind in search of truth, that it would be the TERMINUS AD QAEM in which when it was once attained the mind would finally acquiesce.

Again the obscurity of the text was to be in some measure removed by the annotations of Stella; not however wholly, for Bacon in the epitome of the eighteenth chapter commends the manner of publishing knowledge 'whereby it shall not be to the capacity nor taste of all, but shall as it were single and adopt his reader.' Stella was therefore to throw a kind of starlight on the subject, enough to prevent the student's losing his way, but not much more."

Die andere klassische Interpretation gibt Anderson (op.cit.16/17):

"'The word 'terminus' probably indicates the 'limits and end' to which investigation may proceed. The ANNOTATIONS, of which 'none are set down in this fragments'—to quote a statement written on the manuscript by Bacon's hand, are to throw a light as by a star (STELLA). Now 'star' is the symbol used by Bacon in the GESTA GRAYORUM, the ADVANCEMENT OF LEARNING, and the DE AUGMENTIS to represent the sovereign. And the significance which he attaches to the word 'Hermes' is evident from his address to King James in the Introduction to the ADVANCEMENT OF LEARNING. 'There is met in your Majesty, says Bacon, 'a rare conjunction as well of divine and sacred literature as of profane and human; so as your Majesty standeth invested of that triplicity which in great veneration was ascribed to the ancient Hermes; the power and fortune of a King, the knowledge and illumination of a Priest, and the learning and the universality of a Philosopher.' Bacon is, or pretended to be, greatly impressed by James's learning: 'To drink indeed', he says, 'of the true fountains of learning, nay to have such a fountain of learning in himself, in a king, and in a king born, is always a miracle.' And it would appear that he hopes at the beginning of James's reign—long before he suffers disillusionment respecting his sovereign's interest in the advance of 'solid' knowledge—that, whether or not he can obtain a greater position of state beyond that alloted to him by Elizabeth, he may be enabled to have the modern Hermes, king of the realm and head of the church, and a literary man of no mean fame and importance, annote a subject's work on the new science. James, when he has done this, may well be prevailed upon to make provision for the operation of the new method of knowledge either by subsidizing helpers or by placing at the author's disposal old or new foundations of learning (Works, II, 175, 180; VI, 90, 172; VIII, 396, 401)."

Brandt (op.cit., 54) lehnt diese Interpretation ab: "1. findet sich keine klare Bezeichnung des Königs als eines Sterns, es läßt sich den von Anderson angegebenen Texten nicht entnehmen, daß Stella als Symbol für Jakob I. zu gelten hat. 2. kann nur ein König als Hermes-Trismegistos angesprochen werden (so VIII, 335 und I, 432, nicht in der englischen Fassung III, 263), weil im Namen die Einheit von Priester, Philosoph und

König liegt, aber im Titel unserer Schrift steht nur Hermes, und die Figur des Hermes hat eme vielfältige Bedeutung; Hermes ist der Grenzgott, auf ihn wird schon in dem Wort 'Terminus' des Titels angespielt; weiter ist Hermes der Götterbote, der 'hermeneus' oder Interpret— die Hermesmythologie ist hineingesponnen in die interpretatio naturae, die sich Bacon zur Aufgabe stellt und in seine Rolle als 'keryx´ und `buccinator', als Bote des Friedens (I, 580-581). Man wird also lieber Hermes Stella eine der vielen Masken Bacons sein lassen und sich damit zugleich von der peinlichen Vorstellung befreien, Bacon künde im Titel seines Werkes an, daß der König die Fußnoten dazu verfaßt (eben das folgt aus der Annahme von Anderson)."

Dieser Auseinandersetzung urn die Bedeutung des Titels eine neue Erklärung anzufügen, halte ich, solange keine neuen Dokumente gefunden werden, für wenig sinnvoll. Allein, es sei angemerkt, wollten wir uns mit Brandt von dieser peinlichen Vorstellung bezüglich Bacons Denken und Trachten befreien, so blieben noch genug Peinlichkeiten der Hybris Bacons."

Franz Träger (Hg.), Valerius Terminus. Von der Interpretation der Natur Würzburg: Königshausen und Neumann, 1984,25-26.

in: The Works of Francis Bacon. Faksimile-Neudruck der Ausgabe von Spedding, Ellis und Heath, London 1857-1874, in vierzehn Bänden (Stuttgart/Bad Cannstadt: Friedrich Fromann, Verlag Günther Holzboog, 1963), vol. 3.{3}

3. Franz Träger discovered that the Spedding & Ellis as MS6462 is not correct, in fact it is MS6463. In his opinion Valerius Terminus was written before The Advancement of Learning. Anderson, Farrington and Rossi also have the opinion that it was written in 1603. Stephens in his edition of 1734 uses the same order as the handwritten

copy of Bacon's text. Later editors, including Spedding and Ellis, choose an order which corresponds to Bacon's new order of chapters given in his index. Franz Träger compared the translation of the 11th chapter with the translation of Guiseppe Furlani, DIE ENTSTEHUNG UND DAS WESEN DER BACONISCHEN METHODE in: Archiv für Geschichte der Philosophie, ed. L. Stein, 33. Bd., Berlin, 1921, S.23-47. (1. Teil, 32. Bd., S. 189 ff). Träger has also checked the following Bacon translations:

ESSAYS, übers. von Elisabeth Schücking, Stuttgart, 1970;

NEUES ORGANON DER WISSENSCHAFTEN, übers. von Anton Theobald Brück, Darmstadt, 1981 (Nachdruck der Ausgabe, Leipzig, 1830);

NOVUM ORGANON, übers. von Rudolf Hoffmann, bearb. von Gertraud Korf, hrsg. von Manfred Buhr, Berlin (DDR), 1982.

OF THE INTERPRETATION OF NATURE.

CAP. 1.

Of the limits and end of knowledge. In the divine nature both religion and philosophy hath acknowledged goodness in perfection, science or providence comprehending all things, and absolute sovereignty or kingdom. In aspiring to the throne of power the angels transgressed and fell{4}, in presuming to come within the oracle of knowledge man transgressed and

4. Antje Peters checked the Old Testament and the New Testament on the fall of the angels:

Jesaja 14, 14 Das Judentum ist geprägt von der antithetisch parallelen Vorstellung von Dämonen und Engeln als Schädiger bzw. Helfer des Menschen. Sie wird in der Erzählung vom Engelfall entfaltet.

Das Buch Jesaja (Jes 14,12ff)14:12 Ach, du bist vom Himmel gefallen, du strahlender Sohn der Morgenröte. Zu Boden bist du geschmettert, du Bezwinger der Völker.

14:13 Du aber hattest in deinem Herzen gedacht: Ich ersteige den Himmel; dort oben stelle ich meinen Thron auf, über den Sternen Gottes; auf den Berg der (Götter)versammlung setze ich mich, im äußersten Norden.

14:14 Ich steige weit über die Wolken hinauf, um dem Höchsten zu gleichen.

14:15 Doch in die Unterwelt wirst du hinabgeworfen, in die äußerste Tiefe.

Im AT gehörte Satan zu den "Söhnen Gottes" im himmlischen Hofstaat, wie die wohl alte Vorstellung Ijob 1,6 zeigt.

Das Buch Ijob (Ijob 1,6)1:6 Nun geschah es eines Tages, da kamen die Gottessöhne, um vor den Herrn hinzutreten; unter ihnen kam auch der Satan.

Er gilt als Diener Gottes und verkörpert eine ursprünglich Gott zugeschriebene Funktion. Der von dann von Gott abgefallene und mit seinem Diener aus dem Himmel gestürzte Engelsfürst wird zum Gegner Gottes und Verführer der Menschen.

Auch im NT findet der Teufel als ein oder der Fürst der gefallenen bösen Engel Erwähnung.

Das Evangelium nach Lukas (Lk 10,18)10:18 Da sagte er zu ihnen: Ich sah den Satan wie einen Blitz vom Himmel fallen.

Der zweite Brief an die Korinther (2 Kor 11,14)11:14 Kein Wunder, denn auch der Satan tarnt sich als Engel des Lichts.

Neben den Bibeltexten wird Bacon auch "De Civitate Dei" (Der Gottesstaat) von Aurelius Augustinus, dem größten lateinischen Kirchenlehrer des christlichen Altertums, vorgelegen haben, in der das Thema Engelfall mehrfach unter verschiedenen Gesichtspunkten erwähnt wird. So wird im elften Buch die Situation der Engel besonders beleuchtet.

Buch XI, 11

... Von dieser Erleuchtung haben sich gewisse Engel abgewendet und sich die Auszeichnung eines weisen und seligen Lebens nicht bewahrt, das zweifellos nur das ewige, seiner Ewigkeit sichere und vergewisserte Leben sein kann. Sie besitzen nur noch ein Vernunftleben, wenn auch ein einsichtsloses und derart, daß sie es, selbst wenn sie wollen, nicht verlieren können. ...

Buch XI, 13

... Die sündigen Engel, die durch ihre Schlechtigkeit jenes Lichtes verlustig gingen, haben sie (die Glückseligkeit), wie wir schlüssig folgern müssen, auch bevor sie fielen, nicht gehabt. ...

Buch XI, 19

... Denn diese Scheidung (zwischen Licht und Finsteris) konnte nur er allein treffen, der auch, bevor sie fielen, ihren künftigen Fall vorauswissen kont, und daß sie, des Lichtes der Wahrheit verlustig, im finsteren Hochmut verharren würden.

Buch XI, 33

Daß es aber Engel gibt, die gesündigt haben und in die tiefste Tiefe dieser Welt verstoßen sind, die ihnen zu einer Art von Kerker wurde, darin sie bis zur bevorstehenden letzten Verurteilung am Tage des Gerichtes zu bleiben haben: das offenbart ganz deutlich der Apostel Petrus. Er sagt, daß Gott die sündigen Engel nicht geschont, sondern sie in die finsteren Abgründe der Hölle hinabgestoßen hat, wo die bis zur Bestrafung im Gerichte gefangengehalten werden. ...

... Und da ja Gott, wie geschrieben steht, "den Stolzen widersteht, den Demütigen aber Gnade gibt" (Jak 4,6; 1 Petr 5,5), wohnt die eine (Engelsgenossenschaft) im Himmel der Himmel und ist die andre von dort hinabgestürzt in diesen untersten Lufthimmel, um hier ruhelos in und her zu schwirren.

Buch XXII,1

Gott ist es, der mit dem freiwilligen Sturz der Engel die völlig gerechte Strafe ewiger Unseligkeit verknüpft hat und den übrigen Engeln, die im höchsten Gut verblieben sind, als Lohn für ihr Verbleiben die Sicherheit gewährt hat, daß dieses Verbleiben kein Ende haben wird.

Aufgrund dieser Erkenntnisse zieht Augustin Parallelen zum Leben der Menschen, besonders im 12. Buch:

Buch XII,1

... Während die einen standhaft in dem allen gemeinsamen Gut, das für sie Gott selbst ist, und in seiner Ewigkeit, Wahrheit und Liebe verharren, sind die anderen, von ihrer eigenen Macht berauscht, als wären sie sich selbst ihr Gut , vom höheren, allen gemeinsamen, beseligenden Gut zum eigenen Selbst abgefallen. ...

fell{5}: but in pursuit towards the similitude of God's goodness or love (which is one thing, for love is nothing else but goodness put in motion or applied) neither man or spirit ever hath transgressed, or shall transgress.{6}

The angel of light that was, when he

5. Spedding's footnote:This clause is repeated in the margin, in the transcriber's hand.

6. similarly in: : I.M. Praefatio Sp. I,132, 19-22; AL Sp. III, 12 seq.

(D.A. Sp. I, 742, 1 9 seq. (footnote

presumed before his fall, said within himself, I WILL ASCEND AND BE LIKE UNTO
THE HIGHEST{7}; not God, but the highest. To be like to God in goodness, was no part of his emulation; knowledge, being in creation an angel of light, was not the want which did most solicit him; only because he was a minister he aimed at a supremacy; therefore his climbing or ascension was turned into a throwing down or precipitation.

Man on the other side, when he was tempted before he fell, had offered unto him this suggestion, THAT HE SHOULD BE LIKE UNTO GOD{8}. But how? Not simply, but in this part, KNOWING GOOD AND EVIL. For being in his creation invested with sovereignty of all inferior

taken from the French translation of Valerius Terminus by Francois Vert, Meridiens Klincksieck, 1986)

7. Isaiah 14, 14: Authorized Version: I will ascend above the heights of the clouds; will be like the most high.

8. Genesis 3, 5: Authorized Version: For God does know that in the day ye eat thereof, then your eyes shall be opened, and ye shall be as gods, knowing good and evil.

For Bacon's alleged use of the Geneva Bible see Henri Durel-Leon in Transactions of the Cambridge Bibliographical Society, XI:2 (1997), p. 160 and n. 74, modified in the direction of AV by, probably, Lancelot Andrewes in AL. (Thanks to Dr. Leedham-Green)

Geneva Bible: The First Boke of Moses, called Genesis, Chap 3,4+5: Then the serpent said to the woman, Ye shal not dye at all, But God doeth knowe, that when ye shall eat thereof, your eyes shalbe opened, & ye shalbe as gods knowing good and evil. [footnote c: As thogh he shulde say, God doeth not forbid you to eat of the frute, save that he knoweth that if you shulde eat thereof, you shulde be like to him]

Authorized Version: And the serpent said unto the woman, Ye shall not creatures{9}, he was not needy of power or dominion; but again, being a spirit newly inclosed in a body of earth, he was fittest to be allured with appetite of light and liberty of knowledge; therefore this approaching and intruding into God's secrets and mysteries was rewarded with a further removing and estranging from God's presence. But as to the goodness of God, there is no danger in contending or advancing towards a similitude thereof, as that which is open and propounded to our imagination. For that voice (whereof the heathen and all other errors of religion have ever confessed that it sounds not like man), LOVE YOUR ENEMIES; BE YOU LIKE UNTO YOUR HEAVENLY FATHER, THAT SUFFERETH HIS RAIN TO FALL BOTH UPON

THE JUST AND THE UNJUST{10}, doth well declare, that we can in that point commit no excess; so again we find it often repeated in the old law, BE YOU HOLY AS I AM

surely die: For God doth know that in the day ye eat thereof, then your eyes shall be opened, and ye shall be as gods, knowing good and evil.

Vulgata: dixit autem serpens ad mulierem nequaquam morte moriemini /scit enim Deus quod in quocumque die comederitis ex eo aperientur oculi vestri et eritis sicut dii scientes bonum et malum

9. Genesis I, 1,26 Geneva Bible: Furthermore God said, Let us make man in our image according to our lickeness, and let them rule over the fish of the sea, and over the foule of the heaven, and over the beastes, & over all the earth, and over everiething that crepeth & moveth on earth.

Authorized Version: And God said, Let us make man in our image, after our likeness: and let them have dominion over the fish of the sea, and over the fowl of the air, and over the cattle, and over all the earth, and over every creeping thing that creepeth upon the earth.

Vulgata: Et ait faciamus hominem ad imaginem et similitudinem nostram et praesit piscibus maris et volatilibus caeli et bestiis universaeque terrae omnique reptili quod movetur in terra

10. Matthew 5, 44-45 Geneva Bible: Love your enemies... That you may be the children of your Father that is in heaven: for he maketh his sunne to arise on the evil, and the good, and he sendeth raine on the iuste, & unjuste.

HOLY{11}; and what is holiness else but goodness, as we consider it separate and guarded from all mixture and all access of evil?

Wherefore seeing that knowledge is of the number of those things which are to be accepted of with caution and

distinction{12}; being now to open a fountain, such as it is not easy to discern where the issues and streams thereof will take and fall; I thought it good and necessary in the first place to make a strong and sound head or bank to rule and guide the course of the waters; by setting down this position or firmament{13}, namely, THAT ALL KNOWLEDGE IS TO BE LIMITED BY RELIGION, AND TO BE REFERRED

Authorized Version: Love your enemies:... That you may be the children of your father which is in heaven: for he maketh his sun to rise on the evil and on the good, and sendeth rain on the just and on the unjust.

Vulgata: Ego autem dico vobis diligite inimicos vestros ... ut sitis filii Patris vestri qui in caelis est qui solem suum oriri facit super bonos et malos et pluit super iustos et iniustos.

11. Leviticus 11,44: Authorized Version: For I am the Lord your God: ye shall therefore sanctify yourselves, and ye shall be holy; for I am holy: neither shall ye defile yourself with any manner of creeping thing that creepeth upon the earth. 1 Peter 1, 16:

Authorized Version: For it is written, Be ye holy; for I am holy. see also Leviticus 20,7 and 20,26 12. cf. A.L. Sp.III, 264, 1.18 (D.A. Sp. I, 433, I. 29,30)

13. Melek Hasgün comments: 'Firmament' means, apart from the arch or vault of heaven overhead, in which the clouds and the stars appear, in the literal etymological sense a firm support or foundation. At the beginning of his text Bacon sets the

basis for his further theories. According to Bacon it is important not to try to find out the secrets and mysteries of God or to desire to be like God, as was the case in the Fall of Man and the Fall of Angels. Thus it is forbidden to exceed these limits, but to inquire into nature and its creatures is legitimate, because God has "...let man have dominion over (...) all the earth..."(Gen.I, 1,26). He maintains that all knowledge is limited by religion and by this statement he also avoids any suspicion on heresy, which could arise because of his desire for progress and knowledge.

TO USE AND ACTION{14}.

14. "Ad meritum et usus vitae", Works, vol. I, p. 132 ; Italics in order to stress the importance; probably not a quotation.

For if any man shall think by view and inquiry into these sensible and material things, to attain to any light for the revealing of the nature or will of God, he shall dangerously abuse himself. It is true that the contemplation of the creatures of God hath for end (as to the natures of the creatures themselves) knowledge, but as to the nature of God, no knowledge, but wonder; which is nothing else but contemplation broken off, or losing itself. Nay further, as it was aptly said by one of Plato's school THE SENSE OF MAN RESEMBLES THE SUN, WHICH OPENETH AND REVEALETH THE TERRESTRIAL GLOBE, BUT OBSCURETH AND CONCEALETH THE CELESTIAL{15}; so doth the sense discover natural things, but darken and shut up divine. And this appeareth sufficiently in that there

15. Philo d'Alexandrie, Des Songes, Livre I, 83-4 (footnote taken from the Vert translation)

16. St. Matthew 22, 21: Authorized Version: ... Then saith he unto them, Render therefore unto Caesar the things which are Caesar's; and unto God the things that are God's.

17. cf. A.L. Sp. III,478,1.8 sq. (D.A. Sp. I, 830, I. 24 seq.

is no proceeding in invention of knowledge but by similitude; and God is only self-like, having nothing in common with any creature, otherwise than as in shadow and trope. Therefore attend his will as himself openeth it, and give unto faith that which unto faith belongeth{16}; for more worthy it is to believe than to think or know, considering that in knowledge (as we now are capable of it) the mind suffereth from inferior natures; but in all belief it suffereth from a spirit which it holdeth superior and more authorised than itself.{17}

To conclude, the prejudice hath been infinite that both divine and human knowledge hath received by the intermingling and tempering of the one with the other; as that which hath filled the one full of heresies, and the other full of speculative fictions and Vanities{18}.

But now there are again which in a contrary extremity to those which give to contemplation an over-large scope, do offer too great a restraint to natural and lawful knowledge, being unjustly jealous that every reach and depth of knowledge wherewith their conceits have not been acquainted, should be too high an elevation of man's wit, and a searching and ravelling too far into God's secrets; an opinion that ariseth either of envy (which is proud weakness and to be censured and not confuted), or else of a deceitful simplicity. For if they mean that the ignorance of a

18. similarly: A.L. Sp.III, 350,I.24 seq. (D.A. Sp. I, 545, I.35 swq.) John Channing Briggs ("'Bacon's science and religion", in: THE CAMBRIDGE COMPANION TO BACON, ed. By Markku Peltonen, Cambridge 1996) comments on Bacon's separation of divinity and natural philosophy (quotations in Briggs' text are from THE ADVANCEMENT OF LEARNING):

A longstanding commonplace in Bacon scholarship has been the notion that the Baconian advancement of learning depends upon a strict separation of divinity and natural philosophy. In a number of memorable passages Bacon indeed warns his readers of the dire consequences of confusing divinity with natural science: to combine them, he says, is to confound them. This is supposedly what Plato and the scholastics did, and what Bacon explicitly designs the new learning to overcome. Even the acceptable hybrid "divine philosophy," when it is "commixed together" with natural second cause doth make men more devoutly to depend upon the providence of God, as supposing the effects to come immediately from his hand, I demand of them, as Job demanded of his friends, WILL YOU LIE FOR GOD AS MAN WILL FOR MAN TO

philosophy, leads to "an heretical religion, and an imaginary and fabulous philosophy" (III, 350). According to this emphatic strand of Baconian doctrine, religion that joins with the study of nature is in danger of becoming atheistic, or an enthusiastic rival of the true church. Natural philosophy that traffics unwisely with divinity collapses into idolatry or fakery.

Bacon's exemplum of these abuses in a modern proto-science is the divine philosophy of the Paracelsian school, which seeks "the truth of all natural philosophy in the Scriptures." The Paracelsians mirror and reverse the heresies of pagan pantheism by seeking what is "dead" (mortal or natural) from among the "living" (eternal) truths of divinity, when "the scope or purpose of the Spirit of God is not to express matters of nature in the Scriptures, otherwise than in passage, and for application to man's capacity and to matters moral or divine" (ut 485-6). If we take Thomas Sprat at his word, the Royal Society was founded on generally similar principles. The first corruption of knowledge, he argues, resulted from the Egyptians' concealment of wisdom "as sacred Mysteries." The current age of inquiry benefitted from "the dissolution of the ABBYES, whereby their Libraries came forth into the light, and fell into industrious Mens hands." Surrounded by the warring forces of contrary religions (the society's rooms at Gresham College, London, were occupied by soldiers in 1658), the founders of the Royal Society—according to Sprat's account—were "invincibly arm'd" not only against scholastic Catholicism, but against the "inchantments of ENTHUSIASM" and "spiritual Frensies" that sometimes characterized the Protestant revolutionaries.

In Bacon's project, there is an explicit, delineated role for the study of divinity, which he carefully separates from his own work. Reason is at work "in the conception and apprehension of the mysteries of God to us revealed" and in "the inferring and deriving of doctrine and direction thereupon" (III, 479). In the first instance reason stirs itself only to grasp and illustrate revelation; it does not inquire. This is the foundation of Bacon's distinction between true natural philosophy, which inquires into the world as God's manifestation of his GLORY or power, and true theology, which piously interprets the scripturally revealed meaning of God's inscrutable will. The natural world declares God's glory but not his will (III, 478). Reason's power in theology therefore "consisteth of probation and argument." It formulates doctrine only insofar as God's revelation, largely or wholly through Scripture, makes it possible The Lord "doth grift [graft] his revelations and holy doctrine upon the notions of our reason, and applieth his inspirations to open our understanding" (III, 480). (pp. 172-173)

GRATIFY HIM?{19} But if any man without any sinister humour doth indeed make doubt that this digging further and further into

the mine of natural knowledge{20}

19. Job 13, 7-9:

Authorized Version: Will ye speak wickedly for God? and talk deceitfully for him? Will ye accept his person? will ye contend for God? Is it good that he should search you out? as one man mocketh another, do ye so mock him?

20. This image is also used in A.L. Sp.

is a thing without example and uncommended in the Scriptures, or fruitless; let him remember and be instructed; for behold it was not that pure light of natural knowledge, whereby man in paradise was able to give unto every living creature a name according to his propriety{21}, which gave occasion to the fall; but it was an aspiring desire to attain to that part of moral knowledge which defineth of good and evil, whereby to dispute God's commandments and not to depend upon the revelation of his will, which was the original temptation. And the first holy records, which within those brief memorials of things which passed before the flood entered few things as worthy to be registered but only

III, 351, I, 16 where Bacon refers to Democritus (Vert's footnote)

21. Genesis 2,19-20

Geneva Bible: So the Lord God formed of the earth everie beast of the field, and everie foule of the heaven, & broght them unto the man to se how he wolde call them: for howsoever the man named the living creature, so was the name thereof.The man therefore gave names unto all cattle, and to the foule of the heaven, and to everie beast of the field: but for Adam found he not an help mete for him.

Authorized Version: And out of the ground the Lord God formed every beast of the field, and every fowl of the air; and brought THEM unto Adam to see what he would call them: and whatsoever Adam called every living creature, that WAS the name thereof. And Adam gave names to all cattle, and to the fowl of the air, and to every beast of the field; but for Adam there was not found an help meet for him.

Vulgata:Igitur Dominus Deus de humo cunctis animantibus terrae et universis volatilibus caeli adduxit ea ad Adam ut videret quid vocaret ea /omne enim quod vovavit Adam animae viventis ipsum est nomen eius /appelavitque Adam nominibus suis cuncat animantia / et universa volatilia et omnes bestias terrae / Adam vero non inveniebatur adiutor similis eius

lineages{22} and propagations, yet nevertheless honour the

22. Spedding's footnote: LINAGES in original. See note 3, p. 148

remembrance of the inventor both of music{23} and

works in metal{24}. Moses again (who was the reporter) is said to have been seen in all

the Egyptian learning{25}, which nation was early and leading in matter of

knowledge. And Salomon the king,{26} as out of a branch of his wisdom extraordinarily petitioned and granted from God, is said to have written a natural history of all that is green from the cedar to the moss{27}, (which is but a rudiment between putrefaction and

23. Genesis 4,21:
Authorized Version: And his brother's name was Jubal: he was the father of all such as handle the harp and organ
Vulgata: et nomen fratris eius Iuabal ipse fuit pater canentium cithara et organo

24. Genesis, 4,22:
Authorized Version: And Zillah, she also bare Tubalcain, an instructor of every artificer in brass and iron.
Vulgata: Sella quoque genuit Thubalcain qui fuitmalleator et faber in cuncta opera aeris et ferri.

25. The Acts 7,22:
Authorized Version: And Moses was learned in all the wisdom of the Egyptians, and was mighty in words and deeds.

27. 1 Kings 4, 29-34
Geneva Bible: And God gave Salomon wisdome, und understanding exceeding muche, and a large heart, even as the sand that is on the sea shore. And Salomons wisdome excelled the wisdome of all the children of the East and all the wisdome of Egypt. For he was wiser than anie man.... and he was famous throughout all nacions rounde about. And Salomon spake thre thousand proverbes: and his songs were a thousand and five. And he spake of trees, from the cedar tre that is in Lebanon, even unto the hyssope that springeth out of the wall: he spake also of beastes, and of foules, and of creping things, and of fishes. And there came all the people to heare the wisdome of Salomon, from all Kings of the earth, which had heard of his wisdome.
Authorized Version:And God gave Salomon wisdom and understanding exceeding much, and largeness of

heart, even as the sand that is on the sea shore. And Salomon's wisdom excelled the wisdom of all the children of the east country, and all the wisdom of Egypt. For he was wiser than all men...and his fame was in all nations round about. And he spake three thousands proverbs; and his songs were a thousand and five. And he spake of trees, from the cedar tree that is in Lebanon even unto the hyssop that springeth out of the wall: he spake also of beasts, and of fowl, and of creeping things, and of fishes. And there came all people to hear the wisdom of Salomon. From all kings of the earth, which had heard of his wisdom.

Vulgata: Liber Malachim 4, 29-34: Dedit quoque Deus sapientiam Salomoni et prudentiam multam nimis et latitudinem cordis quasi harenam quae est in litore maris / et praecedebat sapientia Salomonis sapientiam omnium orientalium et Aegyoptorum / et erat sapientia cunctis hominibus.. Et erat nominatus inuniversis gentibus per cicuitum / locutus est quoque Salomon tria milia parabolas et fuerunt carmina eius quinque et mille / et disputavit super lignis a cedro quae est in Libano usque ad hysopum quae egreditur de pariete et disseuit de iumentis et volucribus et reptilibus et piscibus / et veniebant de cunctis populis ad audiendam sapientiam Salomonis et ab universis regibus terrae qui audiebant sapientiam eius

Luther Bible: 1. Könige 5, 9-14

Melek Hasgün comments: The hyssop is mentioned in Shakespeare's OTHELLO I,3: "Sow lettuce, set hyssop and weed up thyme". Hyssop and thyme wer believed to aid the an herb{28},) and also of all that liveth and moveth. And if the book of Job be turned over; it will be found to have much aspersion of natural

growth of each other, one being moist and the other dry. The reason why Bacon used moss instead of hyssop could be that moss is also a moist plant and he chose a expression which is more general or known.

28. The plant mentioned in the Bible is not "moss", but HYSOPPUS OFFICINALIS [in German: JOSEFSKRAUT, KIRCHENSEPPL, EISOP, YSOP)]. "The Greek plant name HÝSSOOPOS is probably derived from Hebrew ESOB (mentioned in the Bible...), although it is not clear whether ESOB referred to the plant called hyssop today. Another explanation gives Arabic AZZOF "holy herb" as the source of the name (cf. French HERBE SACRÉ) (Gernot Katzer Website on Spices). Gernot Katzer in his entry on the pomegranate (http://www-ang.kfunigraz.ac.at/~katzer/germ/index .html) considers the problem of the names of plants in the Bible:

"The pomegranate tree is an ancient cultigen in Western Asia; it is mentioned in the oldest part of the Old Testament (the Pentateuch). Although the Old Testament is not a collection of cooking recipes, it names many plants of everyday or cultic usage in ancient Israel; the New Testament, though, has less descriptive character, and plants are, consequently, named much less frequently.

If one wants to set up a "collection of biblical spices", one must not forget that there are three millennia between the language of the Old Testament and ours; therefore, exact translations are sometimes impossible. The following quote (Isaiah 28,27) may illustrate the difficulties of translation:

'QETSACH is not threshed with a sledge, nor is a cartwheel rolled over KAMMON; QETSACH is beaten out with a rod, and KAMMON with a stick.'

Because of the dialectic structure, we may infer that the two plants are similar, but differ in details of their harvest. The term KAMMON obviously is related to Greek KÝMINON (cumin), but also lies behind English CARAWAY; QETSACH is more difficult to analyze. Probably it means NIGELLA, sometimes also called BLACK CUMIN, whose seeds ripen in a closed capsule, which must first be opened.

Yet in translating the Bible, botanic accuracy is less an aim than general matters of style. "Black cumin" is less elegant than "cumin", and "nigella" is not an English word at all. Therefore, English Bible translations render QETSACH as DILL, CARAWAY or "fitches", a word that is missing from every modern dictionary. German translators, on the other hand, who don't have a traditional, elegant word for CUMIN, commonly translate KAMMON as CARAWAY (which is almost certainly wrong), and have to resort to DILL for QETSACH.

Comparing different translations of the Old Testament, one find some or all of the following (Hebrew terms are given in parenthesis): garlic (shuwm), onion (b@tsel), nigella (qetsach, also rendered as caraway oder dill, quite obscure), cumin (kammon, also caraway), coriander (gad), caper (abiyownah, also translated "desire"), cinnamon (qinnamown), cassia (qiddah, also interpreted as a synonym of cinnamon or cassia buds), hyssop (ezowb, frequent but very obscure), myrtle (hadac), olive (shemen and zayith, very frequent), juniper (b@rowsh, also given as "fir" or "pine"), almond (shaqed), pomegranate (rimmown or rimmon), rose (chabatstseleth, very obscure) and saffron (karkom).

Similarly, the New Testament has not been translated by biologists—the latter had not suspected birds to live in mustard plants (sínapi). Other plant names from the New Testament include the following (Greek given in parenthesis): mint (heedýosmon, this is not the common name of mint in Greek), cumin (kýminon, also translated caraway), anis (áneethon, also rendered dill), rue (peéganon, not the common term), cinnamon (kinnámoomon), hyssop (hýssoopos, referring to the obscure word in the Old Testament) and olive (agriélaios "olive tree" and elaíon "olive oil").

The DICTIONARY OF THE BIBLE (ed. By James Hastings and John A. Selbie, Edinburgh, 3rd ed.1914) says about the HYSSOP: "It was used for sprinkling blood (Ex. 12,22) and in the ritual of the cleansing of lepers (Lv 14,4, Nu 19,6); it was an insignificant plant growing out of the wall (1 K 4,33); it could afford a branch strong enough to support a wet sponge (Jn 19,29). It is possible that all these references are not to a single species. Among many suggested plants the most probable is either a species of majoran, e.g., ORIGANUM MARU, or the common caper-plant (CAPPARIS SPINOSA), which may be seen growing out of crevices in walls all over Palestine" (E.W.G.Masterman).

For the German traditions about the

hyssop Jacob and Wilhem Grimm in
DEUTSCHES WÖRTERBUCH
(1854 seq.) give the following
information: YSOP, isop, ispe(n),
eisop; hysop, m. (F.),HYSSOPUS
OFFICINALIS L., KLEINER
BUSCH MIT STARK
DUFTENDEN BLÄTTERN und
VIOLETTEN BLÜTEN.
GELEGENTLICH WIRD DER
NAME AUF VERWANDTE
PFLANZEN ÜBERTRAGEN, VOR
ALLEM AUF SATUREJA
HORTENSIS L., VGL. MARZELL
WB. D. DT. PFLANZENN. 2, 966
ff.; PRITZEL-JESSEN PFLANZEN
(1882) 363 f.; FISCHER SCHWÄB. 4,
53.
HERKUNFT UND form.
ASS. zûpu; SYR.-ARAB. züfä; HEBR.
.; GRIECH. ; ; LAT. hyss*pus* F.,
*hyss*pum N.; GOT. hwssopon (DAT.
SG.); AGS. ysope f.; AHD. hysop ST.
M. NEBEN SPÄTEREM ISOPO,
isipo 5W. M.; MHD. ysope M.
(NOCH BEI LUTHER MEIST
SCHWACH FLEKTIERT: EXOD.
12, 22; LEVIT. 14, 52; PS. 51, 9;
HEBR. 9, 19); SPÄTAHD.-
FRÜHNHD. AUCH ALS FEM.
(YSOPUS îspa [12. JH.] AH. GL. 3,
264, 53 ST.-S.; DE ISOPO von der
ispen [12.JH.] EBDA 4, 365, 46; von
der ispen [UM 1350] KONRAD V.
MEGENBEEG BUCH D. NATUR
405 PF.; VGL. 420; yspen, die nit felt
LIEDERBUCH D. HÄTZLERIN
234 HALTAUS). NHD. (h)ysop, isop,
WEITERES S.U.
AUF DER BIBELSPRACHLICHEN
TRADITION (1) UND AUF DER
FRÜHEN EINFÜHRUNG DES
ORIENTALISCH-
SÜDEUROPÄISCHEN YSOPS ALS
HEIL- UND GEWÜRZPFLANZE

(2) BERUHT SEINE REICHE BEZEUGUNG IN NAHEZU ALLEN EUROPÄISCHEN SPRACHEN. NEUER- DINGS WIRD DIE IDENTITÄT DES BIBLISCHEN ysop MIT HYSSOPUS OF/ICINALIS WIEDER BEZWEIFELT MARZELL A. A. 0. (ZUR DISKUSSION UM JOAN. 19, 29 VGL. BAUER GRIECH.-DT. WB. ZUM NEUEN TESTAM. [4 1952] 1541). DER NAME ERSCHEINT BIBEL-SPRACHLICH DURCHWEG ALS MASK., GELEGENTLICH BIS INS 14. JH. IN LAT. FLEXIONSFORM (S. U. DAT. SG. isupo NOTKER, ysopo TRIERER PS., ysopo PASSIONAL; AKK. SG.. ysopum WERNHER MARIENLEBEN) UND AUCH SPÄTER NOCH MIT SPIRANTISCHEM ANLAUT: hyssop ABR. A S. CLARA etw. f. alle (1699) 1, 98; hysop BRENNER ERZ. U. SCHR. (1864) 1, 20; hyssop TILLMANN NEUES TEST. (LPZ. 6 1958) 625. WEITER EINGEDEUTSCHT IST DAS WORT IN SEINER VOLKSSPRACHLICHEN VERWENDUNG (2): SYNKOPE DES MITTELSILBENVOKALS S.. OB. SOWIE isp (12. JH.) AHD. GL. 4, 235, 38 ST.-S.; yspe (14. JH.) EBDA 3, 542, 25; ispe (U. Ä.) 14./16. JH. DIEFENBACH GL. 310b ; isp(e) FISCHER SCHWÄB. 4, 53 (STÄRKER ABWEICHENDE MISCHFORMEN zispe EBDA, zwispe 6, 1472), SCHMELLER-FR. BAYER. 1, 168. NICHT SELTEN DIPHTHONGIERT garteneisop, zwibeleisop ALBERTUS dict. (1540) FF la ; eisop FÄBRICUS RER. MISNIAC. (1569) 246; eysopwein

ZEHNER NOMENCL. (1643) 365; eisop M. BÖHME VIEHARTZNEY (1682) 31. DIE ZAHLREICHEN MUNDARTLICHEN NEBENFORMEN S. IM ÜBRIGEN BEI MARZELL A. A. O.; VGL. NOCH eisop TEIL 3, SP. 380, eisewig 3, 377, hispe F., 4, 2, 1579 SOWIE isop 4, 2, 2182.

GEBRAUCH.

1)BIBELSPRACHLICH. EXOD. 12, 22; LEVIT. 14, 4 U. 6; 14, 49fl.; num. 19, 6 u. 18; PS. 50 9 U. HEBR. 9, 19 ERWÄHNEN DEN YSOP IM ZUSAMMENHANG KULTISCHER REINIGUNGSZEREMONIEN. 3. REG. 4, 33 DIENT ER EINEM VERGLEICH ZUR VERANSCHAUIICHUNG DER WEISHEIT SALOMOS (S.U.). JOAN. 19, 29 WIRD DEM GEKREUZIGTEN DER ESSIGSCHWAMM UM EINEN YSOP GEWICKELT GEREICHT (HIERZU VGL. BAUER GRIECH.-DT. WB. ZUM NEUEN TESTAM. [4 1952] 1541). AN DIESEN STELLEN IST DAS WORT IN ALLEN DEUTSCHEN BIBELÜBERSETZUNGEN BIS IN DIE GEGENWART IN FESTEM GEBRAUCH: afaruh þan ÞO in wato wairpandans hrain jah hwssopon jah wullai raudai ufartrusnjandans (SKEIREINS 3, 16) GOT. BIBEL 21 , 461 STREITBERG; FASCICULUM HYSOPI uuadal hysopes (EXODUS 12, 22) (8./9. JH.) AHD. GL. 1, 335, 38 ST.-S.; so er chumet, so besprenget er mih mit isopo (ASPERGES ME YSOPO, PS. 50, 9) also die miselsuhtigen, unde danne uuirdo ih gereinet; uuunda so ist gepoten in demo puoche, daz die miselsuhtigen siben stunt besprenget uurten mit gedunchetemo isopo in demo opferpluote (VGL. LEV. 14, 4ff.; 49ff.) NOTKER 3, 172 PIPER (VGL. 2, 195f.); du besprenges mih, herro, mit dem isipen unde ih wirde gereinet (12. JH., WINDBERGER INTERLINEARVERSION), du solt besprengen mich mit demo ysopo unde ih wirde gereinet (13. JH., TRIERER INTERLINEARVERSION) (PS. 50, 9) DT. INTERLINEARVERSIONEN D. PSALMEN (1839) 232 GRAFF; wann sy fulten ein schwamp mit essig sy vmbgaben in mit ysopp: sy brachten in seinen mund (JOAN. 19, 29) ERSTE DT. BIBEL 1, 415 KURR.; vnd er (SALOMO) redet dreytausent spruch, vnd seyner liede waren tausent vnd funffe. vnd er redet von bewmen, vom ceder an zu Libanon bis an den isop, der aus der wand wechst (3. REG. 4, 33) LUTHER DT. BIBEL 1, 150 W., VGL. 9, 1, 408f. AUS BIBELSPRACHLICHER TRADITION ERWACHSEN FOLGENDE BELEGE, ZU PS. 50, 8:

Maria sunderinne,
du bist in gutem sinne
vf einen burnen alda kumen
...
betouche dich zv male
des du macht Immer wesen vro
der besprenget dich mit ysopo
des bistu wiz ob alleme sne
(UM 1300) PASSIONAL 371, 22 HAHN;

nun spreng mich herr mit ysop gut,
so wird all sünd verderbet
SPEE GÜLD. TUGENDBUCH (1649) 35;

und so, meint der meister ferner, werde ich auch bald gewaschen

werden, und mit hysop besprengt, der
ich über so viele das miserere
gesungen BRENNER ERZ. U.
SCHR. (1864) 1, 20. ZU JOAN. 19,
29:

'mich durstet', sprach er och dar na.
do stûnd ain vas mit essich da,
dar in lait ainer ysopum
und fuitent sin ainen schwum:
den bot er zû der selben stunt
mit ainem sper an sinen munt

(HS. 1182) WERNHER
MARIENLEBEN 10 607 PÄPKE-
HÜBNER.
IN NEGATIVIERENDER
UMDEUTUNG DER
HILFREICHEN TRÄNKUNG AUS
JOAN. 19, 29 (VGL. MATTH. 27,
34): wie . . dem volk...der ysop der
furcht vor den ewigen strafen
dargereicht würde
SCHLEIERMACHER S. W. (1834) 1
5, 98;

nur gift und galle war, o pabst,
was du vom pol bis zu den tropen
der welt mit deinem scepter gabst,
mit deinem scepter von ysopen

HERWEGH GED. E.
LEBENDIGEN (21841) 116.
ZU 3. REG. 4, 31 von der zeder bis
zum ysop (S 0. LUTHERS
ÜBERSETZUNG), ZUNÄCHST
NUR VON DER GRÖSZE DER
WEISHEIT SALOMOS: Salomon ...
von dem ceder baum, so auf dem berg
Libano ist, bisz auf den hyssop, so aus
der wand wächst, disputiert ABR. A
S. CLARA ETWAS F. ALLE (1699)
1, 48; (ÜBERSCHRIFT:) Salomons
königs van Israel und Juda güldne
worte von der ceder biss zum issop
GÖTHE 1 37, 295 W.; AUF
ANDERE PERSONEN
ÜBERTRAGEN: weil du
(RÜBEZAHL) aber der kräuter und

pflanzen kundig bist, vom ysop an, der auf der mauer wächst, bis auf die ceder zu Libanon MUSÄUS VOLKSMÄRCHEN 1, 34 HEMPEL, VGL. DERS., PHYSIOGN. REISEN (1778) 1, 171; ich habe die ehre, ihnen einen gelehrten zu präsentieren, dar alles weiss und kennt, van der ceder bis zum ysop KOTZEBUE SÄMMTL. DRAM. W. (1827) 1, 314. SCHLIESZLICH DIE WEITE DER SCHÖPFUNG ÜBERHAUPT BEZEICHNEND: jedes gewäche von der ceder bis zum ysop hängt an erde und sonnenschein HERDER 20, 73 S.; VGL. 22, 237; der nahme meines helden ist kurz und gut: ABC bis XYZ, ... ritter vieler orden trauriger und fröhlicher gestalt, von der ceder auf Libanon bis zum ysop HIPPEL KREUZ- U. QUERZUGC (1793) 1, 3; die menschengattung ist die erste von alless diesen einheiten; die andern, vom elephanten bis zur milbe, von der ceder bis an den ysop, sind in dar zweiten und dritten linie J. G. FORSTER S. SCHR. (1843) 4, 319. 2) ALS GEWÜRZ- UND HEIL PFLANZE. IN DEN VERSCHIEDENSTEN REZEPTEN SEIT DEM 11./12. JH. SEHR REICH BEZEUGT; DIE BLÄTTER WERDEN VEREINZELT BIS IN DIE GEGENWART ALS SOSZENWÜRZE UND ZUM GURGELN GEGEN HALSBESCHWERDEN BENUTZT; DARÜBER HINAUS IST DIE PFLANZE 'VOR ALLEM IN DER SCHWEIZ EIN BESTANDTEIL DER IN DIE KIRCHE (BESONDERS VON ÄLTEREN FRAUEN) MITGENOMMENEN RIECHSTRÄUSZLEIN' MARZELL

WB. D. DT. PFLANZENN. 2, 069: isopo ist g*t chrût, obe diu geb*rt stirbet in demo wîbe; trinche iz mit warmem wazzer, SÔ vert iz vone ire. er ist g*t vur den stenken vnte hilfet och den der mage swirt (11./12. JH.) GERMANIA 8, 300; ÄHNLICH (13. JH.) MENHARDT VERZ. D. ALTDT. LIT. HSS. 1 (1960) 46; von der ispen. isopus haizt isp...wenn man ispen kocht mit honig, daz ist der lungel guot . und genuog ander tugent hât si an ir (UM 1350) KONRAD V. MEGENBERG BUCH der NATUR 405 PF.; vgl 420; der ysope . . . ist bitter und idoch ges*nt dem herzen und der I*ngen und der b*rst die da siech ist (14 JH.) ALTDT.PRED. SCHÖNBACH SO WEME dat hoven sweret . . de scal nemen eyn bunt ysopen unde seden de (Bremen 1352) »MND. ARZNEIB. des A. DONELDEY 14 Windler vgl. 3, 10, 19, 26, 49; und alz ist gefügett daz pinlin z.B. dem honge, der ysop z.B. dem balsam, dú nahtegal z.B. der harpfen (so wie DIE seele ZU CHRISTUS) (HS. Von 1357 NACH VORLAGE VON 1303) , ST. GEORGENER PRED. 287 RIEDER, VGL. 294;

> saluay, rawtten vnd polay,
> der krautt stünd pogen vnd
> gezindelt;
> dryment, yspen, die nit felt,
> grunten da in reicher wunn

LIEDERBUCH DER HÄTZLERIN 234 HALTAUS: dem rind den husten zu vertreiben, pflegt man jnen...ysop.. .einzugeben SEBIZ feldbau (1579) 128; mit lavendel, isop, majoran, poley und anderen geringeres wehrtes, gewächsen und blurnenwerke ausgeziehret NEUMARK newspross. teut. palmb. (1668) 171; unter wild

wachsenden pflanzen sah ich die
dunkelrote scabiose unter gärten und
ein ganzes feld mit ysop bewachsen
STOLBERG GES.W. (1820) 8, 360.
3) ZU BEIDEN
ANWENDUNGSGRUPPEN
STELLEN SICH
ZUSAMMENSETZUNGEN:
ysopbitter:
dieweil der königliche zecher
umsonst nach ihren zügen gafft.
leert sie den ysopbittren becher
zurückgewiesener leidenschaft
FONTANE GED. 7176 (VGL..
JOAN. 19, 29 u. ysop 1);
—busch:
nimm einen ysoppusch,
entsündige mein Leben
FLEMING, dt. ged. 1,8
lit.ver.;
VGL. ysopbüschel (NURN. 19, 18)
ZÜRCHER BIBEL (BERLIN 1956)
1, 165; - kraut: nimm rosinlin ein
handvoll...salbeyblätter, hissopkraut,
jedes 1 hand voll GÄBELKOVER
ARTZNCYB. (1595) 1, 182; -saft:
ysop safft getruncken mit oximel,
waychet den verstopften bauch DAS
KREÜTERBUCH OD.
HERBARIOS (AUGSB. 1534) 144b ;
-sirup: \STAUB-TOBLER 7, 1270; -
stengel: sie steckten nun einen mit
essig gefüllten schwamm auf einen
ysopstengel (JOAN 19,29).
ZÜRCHER BIBEL (BERLIN 1956)
2,148; hysopstengel (J. 19,29)
TILLMANN NEUES TESTAM.
(LPZ. 6-1959) 325; -strauch, s.
isopstrauch TEIL 4,2, SP. 2182; -
wasser: hysopwasser soll man allwegen
in heysser aeschen distilliren: welches
(U. A.) trefflich gut für den grausamen
schmertzen der zän ist SEBIZ feldbau
(1580) 413; zerschmeltz den zucker in
brandlattich oder issopwasser

GÄBELKOVER artzneybuch (1595) 1, 193, GEBUCHT bei RÄDLEIN T.-IT.-FRZ.(1711) 1080;b; -wein, . VGL. isopwein TEIL 4. 2. sp. 2182 SOWIE: von ysopwein. ysopwein ist warm, reiniget die brust, machet gute däwung vnd weicht den bauch M. HERR FELDBAU (1551) 112a; eysop wein ZEHNER NOMENCL. (1645) 365; KIRSCH CORNU COPIAE 2 (1775), 908.

Why then did Bacon translate "hyssop" as "moss"? The hyssop was known and used in England (compare OED; e.g. Skakespeare OTHELLO I,3 etc.). What appears from all the dictionaries consulted is, however, that it is not so very clear which plant was meant by the name. What led Bacon to use the word "moss" for "hyssop" is probably the sense of 1 K 4,33: Salomon knows every plant from the noblest (=cedar tree) to the meanest (=hyssop), "moss" obviously signifying a mean plant "which is but a rudiment between putrefaction and an herb". This does obviously leave out of consideration the holiness of the hyssop tested in various other contexts of the Old and the New Testament (see above).

philosophy{29}. Nay, the same Salomon the king affirmeth directly that the glory of God IS TO CONCEAL A THING, BUT THE GLORY OF THE KING IS TO FIND IT OUT{30}, as if according to the innocent play of children the divine Majesty took delight to hide his works, to the end to have them found out; for in naming the king he intendeth man, taking such a condition of man as hath most excellency and greatest commandment of wits and means,

29. cf. A.L. Sp. III, 298, I.5 (D.A. Sp.I,467, I.1) ; Cf. also N.O. I, 65
30. Proverbs 25,2
Geneva Bible: The glorie of God is to conceile a thing secret: but the Kings honour is to searche out a thing.
Authorized Version: It is the glory of God to conceal a thing: but the honour
of kings is to search out a matter.
Vulgata: Gloria Dei celare verbum et gloria regum investigare sermonem
31. Proverbs 20,27
Geneva Bible: The light of the Lord is

alluding also to his own person, being truly one of those clearest burning lamps, whereof himself speaketh in another place, when he saith THE SPIRIT OF MAN IS AS THE LAMP OF GOD, WHEREWITH HE SEARCHETH ALL INWARDNESS{31}; which nature of the soul the same Salomon holding precious and inestimable, and therein conspiring with the affection of Socrates who scorned the pretended learned men of his time for raising great benefit of their learning (whereas Anaxagoras contrariwise and divers others being born to ample patrimonies decayed them in

the breth of man, and sercheth all the bowels of the bellie. Authorized Version: The spirit of man is the candle of the Lord,searching all the inward parts of the belly. Vulgata: lucerna Dominis spiraculum homninis quae investigat omnia secreta ventris

Luther: Eine Leuchte des Herrn ist des Menschen Geist; die geht durch alle Kammern des Leibes.

contemplation){32}, delivereth it in precept yet remaining, BUY THE TRUTH, AND SELL IT NOT; AND SO OF WISDOM AND KNOWLEDGE{33}.

32. see Platon, Hippias Major. 282 b - 283 b

33. Proverbs 23, 23

And lest any man should retain a scruple as if this thirst of knowledge were rather an humour of the mind than an emptiness or want in nature and an instinct from God, the same author defineth of it fully, saying, GOD HATH MADE EVERY THING IN BEAUTY ACCORDING TO SEASON; ALSO HE HATH SET THE WORLD IN MAN'S HEART, YET CAN HE NOT FIND OUT THE WORK WHICH GOD WORKETH FROM THE

Geneva Bible: Bye the trueth, but sel it not: likewise wisdome, and instruction, and understanding.

Authorized Version: Buy the truth and sell it not; also wisdom, and instruction, and understanding.

Vulgata: veritatem eme et noli vendere sapientiam et doctrinam et intelligentiam

Luther: Kaufe Wahrheit und verkaufe sie nicht, Weisheit, Zucht und Verstand.

on the mercantilist spirit in Bacon see:

BEGINNING TO THE END{34}: declaring not obscurely that God hath framed the mind of man as a glass capable of the image of the universal world, joying to receive the signature thereof as the eye is of light yea not only satisfied in beholding the variety of things and vicissitude of times, but raised also to find out and discern those ordinances and decrees which throughout all these changes are infallibly observed. And although the highest generality of motion or summary law of nature God should still reserve within his own curtain, yet many and noble are the inferior and secondary operations which are within man's sounding. This is a thing which I cannot tell whether I may so plainly speak as truly conceive, that as all knowledge appeareth to be a plant of God's own planting, so it may seem the spreading and flourishing or at least the bearing and fructifying of this plant, by a providence of God, nay not only by a general providence but by a special prophecy, was appointed to this autumn of the world{35}: for to my understanding it is not violent to the letter, and safe now after the event, so to interpret that place in the prophecy of Daniel where speaking of the latter times it is said, MANY SHALL PASS TO AND FRO, AND SCIENCE SHALL BE INCREASED{36}; as if the opening of the world by navigation and commerce and the further discovery of knowledge

Julie Robin Salomon, Objectivity in the Making. The John Hopkins University Press, 1998.

35. Melek Hasgün comments: Bacon sees his time as "...autumn of the world...". As in Shakespeare's King Lear (IV/6) 'autumn' implies the time shortly before the end of the world, this can also be applied to Bacon. The Apocalypse is preceded by the increase of knowledge (Daniel 12,4) and again Bacon uses the Bible to legitimate progress in science.

36. Daniel 12, 4;
Geneva Bible: But thou, o Daniel, shut up the wordes, and seale the boke til the end of the time: many shal runne

should meet in one time or age.

to and fro, and knowledge shalbe increased [explanation f ("til the end of the time"): Til the time that God hathe appointed for the ful revelation of these things: and then many shal runne to and fro to search the knowledge of these mysteries, which things they obteine now by the light of the Gospel]

But howsoever that be, there are besides the authorities or Scriptures before recited, two reasons of exceeding great weight and force why religion should dearly protect all increase of natural knowledge: the one, because it leadeth the greater exaltation of the glory of God; for as the

Authorized Version: But thou, O Daniel, shut up the words, and seal the book, EVEN to the time of the end: many shall run to and fro, and knowledge shall be increased.

Vulgata: Tu autem Danihel clude sermones et signa librum usque ad tempus statutum / pertransibunt plurimi et multiplex erit scientia
This quotation is repeated on the title page of NOVUM ORGANUM. Together with the allegorical content of the pillars of Hercules, this passage clearly is to be interpreted in an apocalyptical sense: The time has come and is ripe for a re-construction of Adams's paradisical dominion over the world.—The pillars of Hercules can also be understood as a typological allusion to the two pillars of Salomo's temple (cf. Charles Whitney): In 1 Kings 7, 21 the names of the pillars are given as "Jachin" and "Boas". The Jew's name in NOVA ATLANTIS, Joabin, can be explained as the result of playing around with these names and contracting them into one. In NOVA ATLANTIS Salomo's Temple is resurrected and is the centre of knowledge and power.

Psalms{37} and other Scriptures do often invite us to consider and to

37. for example Psalms 19,1

magnify the great and wonderful works of God, so if we should rest only in the contemplation of those shews which first offer themselves to our senses, we should do a like injury to the majesty of God, as if we should judge of the store of some excellent jeweller by that only which is set out to the street in his shop. The other reason is, because it is a singular help and a preservative against unbelief and error; for, saith our Saviour, YOU ERR, NOT KNOWING THE SCRIPTURES NOR THE POWER OF GOD;{38} laying before us two books or volumes to study if we will be secured from error; first the Scriptures revealing the will of God, and then the creatures expressing his power; for that latter book will certify us that nothing which the first teacheth shall be thought impossible. And most sure it is, and a true conclusion of experience, that a little natural philosophy inclineth the mind to atheism, but a further proceeding bringeth the mind back to religion.

38. St. Matthew 22, 29:
Authorized Version: Jesus answered and said unto them, Ye do err, not knowing the Scriptures, not the power of God. see also St Mark 12, 24

To conclude then, let no man presume to check the liberality of God's gifts, who, as was said, HATH SET THE WORLD IN MAN'S HEART. So as whatsoever is not God but parcel of the world, he hath fitted it to the comprehension of man's mind, if man will open and dilate the powers of his understanding as he may.{39}

39. Compare to "mind of glass" above

But yet evermore it must be remembered that the least part of knowledge passed to man by this so large a charter from God must be

40. 1 Corinthians 8, 1
Authorized Version: Now as touching things offered unto idols, we know that we all have knowledge.

subject to that use for which God hath granted it; which is the benefit and relief of the state and society or man; for otherwise all manner of knowledge becometh malign and serpentine, and therefore as carrying the quality of the serpent's sting and malice it maketh the mind of man to swell; as the Scripture saith excellently, KNOWLEDGE BLOWETH UP, BUT CHARITY BUILDETH UP{40}. And again the same author doth notably disavow both power and knowledge such as is not dedicated to goodness or love, for saith he, IF I HAVE ALL FAITH SO AS I COULD REMOVE MOUNTAINS, (there is power active,) IF I RENDER MY BODY TO THE FIRE, (there is power passive,) IF I SPEAK WITH THE TONGUES OF MEN AND ANGELS, (there is knowledge, for language is but the conveyance of knowledge,) ALL WERE NOTHING{41}.

And therefore it is not the pleasure of curiosity{42}, nor the quiet of resolution, nor the raising of the spirit, nor victory of wit, nor faculty of speech, nor lucre of profession, nor ambition of honour or fame, nor inablement for business, that are the true ends of knowledge; some of these being more worthy than other, though all inferior and degenerate: but it is a restitution and reinvesting (in great part) of man to the sovereignty and power (for whensoever he shall be able to call the creatures by their true names be shall again command them) which he had

Knowledge puffeth up, but charity edifieth.

41. 1 Corinthians 13, 1-3:
Authorized Version: Though I speak with the tongues of men and of angels, and have not charity, I am become as sounding brass, or a tinkling cymbal. And though I have the gift of prophecy, and understand all mysteries, and all knowledge; and though I have all faith, so that I could remove mountains, and have not charity, I am nothing. And though I bestow all my goods to feed the poor, and though I give my body to be burned, and have not charity, it profiteth me nothing.

42. Bacon here contrasts "curiosity" with "thirst of knowledge" (p. 220). "Curiosity" is used in a traditional sense (see St. Augustine on curiositas in Confessiones X,35). He speaks of curiositas also in "Actaeon et Pentheus, sive Curiositas" in: De sapentia veterum", VI: The Theban king Pentheus is punished with madness because out of curiosity he has dared to observe certain mysteries which are dedicated to Dionysos, that is: he applied (scientific) observation to divine things, he did not respect the division between LUMEN NATURALE and LUMEN

in his first state of creation{43}. And to speak plainly and clearly, it is a discovery of all operations and pos-sibilities of operations from immortality (if it were possible) to the meanest mechanical practice. And therefore knowledge that tendeth but to satisfaction is but as a courtesan, which is for pleasure and not for fruit or generation. And knowledge that tendeth to profit or profession or glory is but as the golden ball thrown before Atalanta{44}, which while she goeth aside and stoopeth to take up she hindereth the

DIVINUM.—Bacon draws the same conclusions from the myth of Prometheus ("Prometheus, sive Status hominis").

on curiosity see Hans Blumenberg, "Der Prozeß der theoretischen Neugierde", in: DIE LEGITIMITÄT DER NEUZEIT (Frankfurt, 1966).

43. compare with Milton's Paradise Lost Book XII

44. The Atalanta myth is treated by Bacon in DE SAPIENTIA VETERUM (Works, vol. VI)

This is the German translation by Marina Münkler in: Weisheit der Alten, hrsg. von Philipp Rippel (Frankfurt a.M: Fischer, 1991): XXV. Atalanta oder die Gewinnsucht Atalanta, die für ihre Schnelligkeit berühmt war, forderte Hippomenes mit dem Versprechen zum Wettlauf heraus, daß er sie im Falle seines Sieges zur Frau nehmen dürfe, im Falle seiner Niederlage aber sein Leben verwirke. An Atalantas Sieg schien es keinen Zweifel geben zu können, da ihre unübertreffliche Schnelligkeit bereits durch den Tod zahlreicher Freier unter Beweis gestellt worden war. Hippomenes griff deshalb zu einer List. Er beschaffte sich drei goldene Äpfel, die er mit sich führte. Das Rennen begann, Atalanta ging in Führung. Als Hippomenes sah, daß er zurückfiel, griff er auf seine List zurück und warf einen seiner Äpfel so vor sie hin, daß sie ihn sehen mußte. Er warf ihn aber nicht direkt vor sie, sondern ein wenig abseits, damit sie sich nicht nur bücken, sondern auch ihre Bahn verlassen mußte. Erfüllt von weiblicher Gier und angezogen von der Schönheit der Frucht, verließ sie ihre Bahn, lief dem Apfel nach und hielt an, um ihn aufzuheben. In der Zwischenzeit lief Hippomenes weiter und ging in Führung. Aufgrund ihrer natürlichen Schnelligkeit machte Atalanta den Rückstand jedoch bald wieder wett und überholte ihn erneut. Nachdem Hippomenes sie jedoch in derselben Weise noch ein zweites und ein drittes Mal vom Weg abbrachte, gewann er schließlich den Wettlauf, freilich nicht durch seine Fähigkeit, sondern durch seine List.

Diese Sage scheint eine hervorragende Allegorie über den Wettstreit von Kunst und Natur zu sein. Denn die Kunst, die von Atalanta repräsentiert wird, ist an sich, wenn ihr nichts im Wege steht, sehr viel schneller als die Natur, sie ist, wie man sagen könnte, der bessere Läufer und erreicht ihr Ziel schneller. Das zeigt sich an nahezu allen Dingen: Man sieht, daß sich Obstbäume nur langsam aus dem Kern, aber sehr viel schneller durch das Aufpfropfen von Zweigen entwickeln, daß Lehm sehr langsam zu Stein wird, während er sehr schnell zu Stein gebrannt werden kann. Auch die Sitten betreffend kann man beobachten, daß es sehr lange dauert, bis durch die Wohltaten der Natur ein Schmerz vergessen und Trost gefunden werden kann, während die Philosophie (die gleichsam die Kunst zu leben ist), den Tag nicht abwartet,

sondern ihn vorhersieht und vor Augen führt. Dann aber wird dieser Vorsprung und die Fähigkeit der Kunst zum unendlichen Nachteil der Menschheit, durch jene goldenen Äpfel behindert. Denn es gibt keine Wissenschaft oder Kunst, die ihren wahren und richtigen Weg bis zum Ziel unbeirrt beibehält. Vielmehr geschieht es fortwährend, daß die Künste ihre Unternehmungen auf halbem Wege unterbrechen, vom Pfad abweichen und sich wie Atalanta Gewinn und Nutzen zuwenden:
"Declinat cursus, aurumque volubile tollit" (Ovid, Metamorphosen X, 667). Und deshalb ist es nicht verwunderlich, daß es der Kunst nicht gegeben ist, den Sieg über die Natur zu erringen und sie nach den Bedingungen und Regeln des Wettkampfs zu töten und zu zerstören, sondern sie im Gegenteil der Natur unterworfen bleibt, wie das Weib dem Ehemann.

Charles W. Lemmi (THE CLASSICAL DEITIES IN BACON. A STUDY IN MYTHOLOGICAL SYMBOLISM, Baltimore 1933, repr. New York 1971) says that Bacon draws on Natalis Comes (Conti) MYTHOLOGIAE SIVE EXPLICATIONUM FABULARUM LIBRI X (1551) and on Boccaccios DE GENEALOGIA DEORUM (1472).

Simone Wirthmann comments: Treatises on classical mythology had a wide circulation during the Renaissance because it has been thought that one might discover in the stories of the gods and goddesses the wisdom of the ancients. It was in Italy, in the sixteenth century that the Renaissance produced the most widely known works on the classic deities.

One of the most popular books was Natalis Conti's "MYTHOLOGY", which was fully as learned as any of its competitors, pleasanter to read and incomparably easier to use as a referencebook. Furthermore, it systematically interprets every myth it relates according to a multitude of authorities. It provides a list of authorities, an excellent index and synopses of the interpretations divided into ethical and physical. Despite all these new books, which largely superseded Boccaccio's famous "DE GENEALOGIIS DEORUM", they were far from causing it to be forgotten.

For that reason it is to presume that Bacon draws on Natalis Comes (Conti) "MYTHOLOGIAE SIVE EXPLICATIONEM FABULARUM LIBRI X" (1551) and on "Boccaccio's De Genealogia Deorum"(1472) (see Charles W. Lemmi THE CLASSICAL DEITIES IN BACON. A STUDY IN MYTHOLOGICAL SYMBOLISM (Baltimore 1933, repr. New York 1971).

race{45}. And knowledge referred to some particular point of use is but as Harmodius{46} which putteth down one tyrant, and not like

45. Ovid, Metamorphosen, Buch X, 665 680

46. see Herodot, Histories, V, 55 and VI, 109 and 123 The Oxford Classical Dictionary says: Aristogiton (6th c. B.C.), Athenian tyrannicide. He and Harmodius, both of noble family, planned to kill the tyrant Hippias and his younger brother Hipparchus, in consequence of a private quarrel (514 B.C.). The plot miscarried: only Hipparchus was killed. Harmodius was at one cut down by Hippias' guards, Aristogiton arrested and executed (after torture, it is said). As the tyranny was overthrown three years later, the

two were popularly supposed to have made this possible, and were ever after called the Liberators. Simonides wrote a poem in their honour, statues of them were set up in the agora (and new ones erected when these were carried off by Xerxes in 480), and their descendants for all time honoured with the right to meals in the Prytaneum.

Hercules{47} who did perambulate the world to suppress tyrants and giants and monsters in every

47. Hercules is not a Baconian hero. The real hero is Orpheus as he is interpreted in "Orpheus, sive Philosophia" in DE SAPIENTIA VETERUM. Orpheus is the Baconian philosopher, and the myth of Orpheus is about the opera scientiae. The works of Orpheus are superior to the works of Hercules as the "works of wisdom" (opera sapientiae) are superior to the "works of strength" (opera fortitudinis) (VI, 720).

Simone Wirthmann comments: Hercules (gr. Heracles), (lit. "having or showing the glory of Hera"; Hera, wife of Zeus) Hercules, the son of Zeus and of the mortal Alkmene was a celebrated hero of Greek and Roman mythology, who after death was ranked among the gods and received divine honours. He is represented as possessed of prodigious strength, whereby he was enabled to perform twelve extraordinary tasks or "labours" imposed upon him by Hera. One of these tasks was to capture the cattles of the three-headed giant Geryoneus. It is said, that on this journey Hercules set up the rocks Calpé (now Gibraltar) and Abyla (Ceuta) / THE PILLARS OF HERCULES on either side of the Strait of Gibraltar, as a sign for his longest journey. THE PILLARS where seen by the ancients to be the supports of the western boundary of the world.

Bacon uses the myth of Hercules and Harmodius in a methaphorical way, to elucidate the real contents of knowledge by comparing the two "heroes". Hercules impersonates strength and justice, throughout his life he tried to free people from tyranny, fought against giants and monsters without thinking of his own benefit. Harmodius in comparison tried to kill the tyrants Hippias and Hipparchus in consequence of a private quarrel and not primarily to free people.

Bacon uses the myth of Hercules and Harmodius in a methaphorical way, to elucidate the real contents of knowledge by comparing the two "heroes". Hercules impersonates strength and justice, throughout his life he tried to free people from tyranny, fought against giants and monsters without thinking of his own benefit. Harmodius in comparison tried to kill the tyrants Hippias and Hipparchus in consequence of a private quarrel and not primarily to free people.

This shows, that for Bacon knowledge must be of general existence and not only refer to some particular point.

Nevertheless, in one of his later works, DE SAPIENTIA VETERUM (1609), Hercules is not the Baconian hero anymore. The real hero is Orpheus, the philosopher. His works are superior to the works of Hercules as the "works of wisdom" (opera sapientiae) are superior to the "works of strength" (opera fortitudinis) (VI, 729).

Orpheus was a legendary poet, a famous musician and singer of ancient

Greece, who had the power of charming all animate and inanimate objects (he could move rocks and trees) by the sweet strains of his lyre. He descended living into Hades, to bring back to life his wife Eurydice, and perished, torn to pieces by infuriated Thracian maenads (see THE OXFORD CLASSICAL DICTIONARY; THE CENTURY DICTIONARY, VOL. 4)

part.{48} It is true, that in two points the curse is peremptory and not to be removed; the one that vanity must be the end in all human effects, eternity being resumed, though the revolutions and periods may be delayed{49}. The other that the consent of the creature being now turned into reluctation, this power cannot otherwise be exercised and administered but with labour, as well in inventing as in executing; yet nevertheless chiefly that labour and travel which is described by the sweat of the brows more than of the body; that is such travel as is joined with the working and discursion of the spirits in the brain: for as Salomon saith excellently, THE FOOL PUTTETH TO MORE STRENGTH, BUT THE WISE MAN CONSIDERETH WHICH

48. Spedding's note: The words "that is, man's miseries and necessities," which followed in the transcript, have a line drawn through them.

49. Melek Hasgün comments: "...eternity being resumed...".: In Henry VIII (..) and King Lear (I/4) 'resume' means: to take back something previously given or granted. The fact that it is written in the passive form without an object implies that eternity has been taken back by God, referring to the Fall of Man and Paradise Lost.

'Revolution' is the action or fact, on the part of celestial bodies, of moving round in an orbit or circular course. The time in which a planet or other heavenly body completes a full circuit or course. (OED) A look at the complete works and consequences of his work, namely the foundation of scientific or academic institutions after his death that were the precursors of the Royal Society (1660), 'revolution'

WAY{50}, signifying the election of the mean to be more material than the multiplication of endeavour. It is true also that there is a limitation rather potential than actual, which is when the effect is possible, but the time or place yieldeth not the matter or basis whereupon man should work. But notwithstanding these precincts and bounds, let it be believed, and appeal thereof made to TIME, (with renunciation nevertheless to all the vain and abusing promises of Alchemists and Magicians, and such like light, idle, ignorant, credulous, and fantastical wits and sects,) that the new-found world of land was not greater addition to the ancient continent than there remaineth at this day a world of inventions and sciences unknown, having respect to those that are known, with this difference, that the ancient regions of knowledge will seem as barbarous compared with the new, as the new regions of people seem barbarous compared to many of the old.

The dignity of this end (of endowment of man's life with new commodities) appeareth by the estimation that antiquity made of such as guided thereunto. For whereas founders of states,

can also be understood in the modern sense. In fact, NEW ATLANTIS and NOVUM ORGANUM set the foundation for the "intellectual revolution" (Harvey Wheeler's essay on Nova Atlantis; to be obtained from the author: verulan@mindspring.com), which implies the complete overthrow of established state of affairs. (OED)

50. Ecclesiastes 10, 12: Authorized Version: The words of a wise man's mouth are gracious; but the lips of a fool will swallow up himself.
for a commentary see A.L. Sp.III,322, I.14 seq. (D.A. Sp. I, 486, I, 11 seq.)

51. 1 Kings 19,12 (Vulgata)

lawgivers, extirpers of tyrants, fathers of the people, were honoured but with the titles of Worthies or Demigods, inventors were ever consecrated amongst the Gods themselves. And if the ordinary ambitions of men lead them to seek the amplification of their own power in their countries, and a better ambition than that hath moved men to seek the amplification of the power of their own countries amongst other nations, better again and more worthy must that aspiring be which seeketh the amplification of the power and kingdom of mankind over the world; the rather because the other two prosecutions are ever culpable of much perturbation and injustice; but this is a work, truly divine which cometh IN AURA LENI {51} without noise or observation{52}.

The access also to this work hath been by that port or passage, which the divine Majesty (who is unchangeable in his ways) doth infallibly continue and observe; that is the felicity wherewith he hath blessed an humility of mind, such as rather laboureth to spell and so by degrees to read in the volumes of his creatures, than to solicit and urge and as it were to invocate a man's own spirit to divine and give oracles unto him. For as in the inquiry of divine truth, the pride of man hath ever inclined to leave the oracles of God's word and to vanish in the mixture of their own inventions; so in the self-same manner, in inquisition of nature they have ever left the oracles of God's works, and adored the

52. St Luke 17,20:
Authorized Version: And when he was demanded of the Pharisees, when the kingdom of God should come, he answered them and said, The kingdom of God cometh not with observation.

see Novum Organum. I, 93; A.L. Sp. III, 301,I, 29-302; also N.O. I, 129 (Sp. I,222,I.16 seq.)

deceiving and deformed imagery which the unequal mirrors of their own minds have represented unto them{53}. Nay it is a point fit and necessary in the front and beginning of this work without hesitation or reservation to be professed, that it is no less true in this human kingdom of knowledge than in God's kingdom of heaven, that no man shall enter into it EXCEPT HE BECOME FIRST AS A LITTLE CHILD.

53. compare this with the later idea of Idols

54. Spedding's note: This chapter ends at the top of a new page. The rest is left blank.

55. In NO Bacon says that entrance into the new sciences depends upon their followers' imitating the little children favoured by Christ, children whose lack of vanity gives them privileged access to the kingdom of heaven (IV, 69). cf. John Channing Briggs, "Bacon's science and religion", in: THE CAMBRIDGE COMPANION TO BACON, ed. by Markku Peltonen (Cambridge, 1966), 172-199. St Mark, 10,15: Authorized Version: Verily I say unto you, Whosoever shall not receive the kingdom of God as a little child, he shall not enter therein.

CAP. 4.

Of The Impediments Of Knowledge, Being The 4th Chapter, The Preface Only Of It.

In some things it is more hard to attempt than to achieve, which falleth out when the difficulty is not so much in the matter or subject, as it is in the crossness and indisposition of the mind of man to think of any such thing, to will or to resolve it. And therefore Titus Livius in his declamatory digression wherein he doth depress and extenuate the honour of Alexander's conquests saith, NIHIL ALIUD QUAM BENE AUSUS VANA CONTEMNERE: in which sort of things it is the manner of men first to wonder that any such thing should be possible, and after it is found out to wonder again how the world should miss it so long. Of this nature I take to be the invention and discovery of knowledge, etc.

The Impediments Which Have Been In The Times, And In Diversion Of Wits, Being The 5th Chapter, A Small Fragment In The Beginning Of That Chapter.

The encounters of the times have been nothing favourable and prosperous for the invention of knowledge; so as it is not only the daintiness of the seed to take, and the ill mixture and unliking of the ground to nourish or raise this plant, but the ill season also of the weather by which it hath been checked and blasted. Especially in that the seasons have been proper to bring up and set forward other more hasty and indifferent plants, whereby this of knowledge bath been starved and overgrown; for in the descent of times always there hath been somewhat else in reign and reputation, which hath generally aliened and diverted wits and labours from that employment.

For as for the uttermost antiquity which is like fame that muffles her head and tells tales, I cannot presume much of it; for I would not willingly imitate the manner of those that describe maps, which when they come to some far countries whereof they have no knowledge, set down how there be great wastes and deserts there: so I am not apt to affirm that they knew little, because what they knew is little known to us. But if you will judge of them by the last traces that remain to us, you will conclude, though not so scornfully as Aristotle doth, that saith our ancestors were extreme gross, as those that came newly from being moulded out of the clay or some earthly substance; yet reasonably and probably thus, that it was with them in matter of knowledge but as the dawning or break of day. For at that time the world was altogether home-bred, every nation looked little beyond their own confines or territories, and the world had no through lights then, as it hath had since by commerce and navigation, whereby there could neither be that contribution of wits one to help another, nor that variety of particulars for the correcting of customary conceits.

And as there could be no great collection of wits of several parts or nations, so neither could there be any succession of wits of several times, whereby one might refine the other, in regard they had not history to any purpose. And the manner of their traditions was utterly unfit and unproper for amplification of knowledge. And again the studies of those times, you shall find, besides wars, incursions, and rapines, which were then almost every where betwixt states adjoining (the use of leagues and confederacies being not then known), were to populate by multitude of wives and generation, a thing at this day in the waster part of the West-Indies principally affected; and to build sometimes for habitation towns and cities, sometimes for fame and memory monuments, pyramids, colosses, and the like. And if there happened to rise up any more civil wits; then would he found and erect some new laws, customs, and usages, such as now of late years, when the world was revolute almost to the like rudeness and obscurity, we see both in our own nation and abroad many examples of, as well in a number of tenures reserved upon men's lands, as in divers customs of towns and manors, being the devices that such wits wrought upon in such times of deep ignorance, etc.

The Impediments Of Knowledge For Want Of A True Succession Of Wits, And That Hitherto The Length Of One Man's Life Hath Been The Greatest Measure Of Knowledge, Being The 6th Chapter, The Whole Chapter.

In arts mechanical the first device comes shortest and time addeth and perfecteth. But in sciences of conceit the first author goeth furthest and time leeseth and corrupteth. Painting, artillery, sailing, and the like, grossly managed at first, by time accommodate and refined. The philosophies and sciences of Aristotle, Plato, Democritus, Hippocrates, of most vigour at first, by time degenerated and imbased. In the former many wits and industries contributed in one: In the latter many men's wits spent to deprave the wit of one.

The error is both in the deliverer and in the receiver. He that delivereth knowledge desireth to deliver it in such form as may be soonest believed, and not as may be easiliest examined. He that receiveth knowledge desireth rather present satisfaction than expectant search, and so rather not to doubt than not to err. Glory maketh the author not to lay open his weakness, and sloth maketh the disciple not to know his strength.

Then begin men to aspire to the second prizes; to be a profound interpreter and commenter, to be a sharp champion and defender, to be a methodical compounder and abridger. And this is the unfortunate succession of wits which the world hath yet had, whereby the patrimony of all knowledge goeth not on husbanded or improved, but wasted and decayed. For knowledge is like a water that will never arise again higher than the level from which it fell; and therefore to go beyond Aristotle by the light of Aristotle is to think that a borrowed light can increase the original light from whom it is taken. So then no true succession of wits having been in the world, either we must conclude that knowledge is but a task for one man's life, and then vain was the complaint that LIFE IS SHORT, AND ART IS LONG: or else, that the knowledge that now is, is but a shrub, and not that tree which is never dangerous, but where it is to the purpose of knowing Good and Evil; which desire ever riseth upon an appetite to elect and not to obey, and so containeth in it a manifest defection.

CAP. 7.

That The Pretended Succession Of Wits Hath Been Evil Placed, For Asmuch As After Variety Of Sects And Opinions, The Most Popular And Not The Truest Prevaileth And Weareth Out The Rest; Being The 7th Chapter; A Fragment.

It is sensible to think that when men enter first into search and inquiry, according to the several frames and compositions of their understanding they light upon different conceits, and so all opinions and doubts are beaten over, and then men having made a taste of all wax weary of variety, and so reject the worst and hold themselves to the best, either some one if it be eminent, or some two or three if they be in some equality, which afterwards are received and carried on, and the rest extinct.

But truth is contrary, and that time is like a river which carrieth down things which are light and blown up, and sinketh and drowneth that which is sad and weighty. For howsoever governments have several forms, sometimes one governing, sometimes few, sometimes the multitude; yet the state of knowledge is ever a DEMOCRATIE, and that prevaileth which is most agreeable to the senses and conceits of people. As for example there is no great doubt but he that did put the beginnings of things to be SOLID, VOID, AND MOTION TO THE CENTRE, was in better earnest than he that put MATTER, FORM, AND SHIFT; or he that put the MIND, MOTION, AND MATTER. For no man shall enter into inquisition of nature, but shall pass by that opinion of Democritus, whereas he shall never come near the other two opinions, but leave them aloof for the schools and table-talk. Yet those of Aristotle and Plato, because they be both agreeable to popular sense, and the one was uttered with subtilty and the spirit of contradiction, and the other with a stile of ornament and majesty, did hold out, and the other gave place, etc.

CAP. 8.

Of The Impediments Of Knowledge In Handling It By Parts, And In Slipping Off Particular Sciences From The Root And Stock Of Universal Knowledge, Being The 8th Chapter, The Whole Chapter.

Cicero, the orator, willing to magnify his own profession, and thereupon spending many words to maintain that eloquence was not a shop of good words and elegancies but a treasury and receipt of all knowledges, so far forth as may appertain to the handling and moving of the minds and affections of men by speech, maketh great complaint of the school of Socrates; that whereas before his time the same professors of wisdom in Greece did pretend to teach an universal SAPIENCE and knowledge both of matter and words, Socrates divorced them and withdrew philosophy and left rhetoric to itself, which by that destitution became but a barren and unnoble science. And in particular sciences we see that if men fall to subdivide their labours, as to be an oculist in physic, or to be perfect in some one title of the law, or the like, they may prove ready and subtile, but not deep or sufficient, no not in that subject which they do particularly attend, because of that consent which it hath with the rest. And it is a matter of common discourse of the chain of sciences how they are linked together, insomuch as the Grecians, who had terms at will, have fitted it of a name of CIRCLE LEARNING. Nevertheless I that hold it for a great impediment towards the advancement and further invention of knowledge, that particular arts and sciences have been disincorporated from general knowledge, do not understand one and the same thing which Cicero's discourse and the note and conceit of the Grecians in their word CIRCLE LEARNING do intend. For I mean not that use which one science hath of another for ornament or help in practice, as the orator hath of knowledge of affections for moving, or as military science may have use of geometry for fortifications; but I mean it directly of that use by way of supply of light and information which the particulars and instances of one science do yield and present for the framing or correcting of the axioms of another science in their very truth and notion. And therefore that example of OCULISTS and TITLE LAWYERS doth come nearer my conceit than the other two; for sciences distinguished have a dependence upon universal knowledge to be augmented and rectified by the superior light thereof, as well as the parts and members of a science have upon the MAXIMS of the same science, and the mutual light and consent which one part receiveth of another. And therefore the opinion of Copernicus in astronomy, which astronomy itself cannot correct because it is not repugnant to any of the appearances, yet natural philosophy doth correct. On the other side if some of the ancient philosophers had been perfect in the observations of astronomy, and had called them to counsel when they made their principles and first axioms, they would never have divided their philosophy as the Cosmographers do their descriptions by globes, making one philosophy for heaven and another for under heaven, as in effect they do.

So if the moral philosophers that have spent such an infinite quantity of debate touching Good and the highest good, had cast their eye abroad upon nature and beheld the appetite that is in all things to receive and to give; the one motion affecting preservation and the other multiplication; which appetites are most evidently seen in living creatures in the pleasure of nourishment and generation; and in man do make the aptest and most natural division of all his desires, being either of sense of pleasure or sense of power; and in the universal frame of the world are figured, the one in the beams of heaven which issue forth, and the other in the lap of the earth which takes in: and again if they had observed the motion of congruity or situation of the parts in respect of the whole, evident in so many particulars; and lastly if they had considered the motion (familiar in attraction of things) to approach to that which is higher in the same kind; when by these observations so easy and concurring in natural philosophy, they should have found out this quaternion of good, in enjoying or fruition, effecting or operation, consenting or proportion, and approach or assumption; they would have saved and abridged much of their long and wandering discourses of pleasure, virtue, duty, and religion. So likewise in this same logic and rhetoric, or arts of argument and grace of speech, if the great masters of them would but have gone a form lower, and looked but into the observations of Grammar concerning the kinds of words, their derivations, deflexions, and syntax; specially enriching the same with the helps of several languages, with their differing proprieties of words, phrases, and tropes; they might have found out more and better footsteps of common reason, help of disputation, and advantages of cavillation, than many of these which they have propounded. So again a man should be thought to dally, if he did note how the figures of rhetoric and music are many of them the same. The repetitions and traductions in speech and the reports and hauntings of sounds in music are the very same things. Plutarch hath almost made a book of the Lacedaemonian kind of jesting, which joined ever pleasure with distaste. SIR, (saith a man of art to Philip king of Macedon when he controlled him in his faculty,) GOD FORBID YOUR FORTUNE SHOULD BE SUCH AS TO KNOW THESE THINGS BETTER THAN I. In taxing his ignorance in his art he represented to him the perpetual greatness of his fortune, leaving him no vacant time for so mean a skill. Now in music it is one of the ordinariest flowers to fall from a discord or hard tune upon a sweet accord. The figure that Cicero and the rest commend as one of the best points of elegancy, which is the fine checking of expectation, is no less well known to the musicians when they have a special grace in flying the close or cadence. And these are no allusions but direct communities, the same delights of the mind being to be found not only in music, rhetoric, but in moral philosophy, policy, and other knowledges, and that obscure in the one, which is more apparent in the other, yea and that discovered in the one which is not found at all in the other, and so one science greatly aiding to the invention and augmentation of another. And therefore without this intercourse the axioms of sciences will fall out to be neither full nor true; but will be such opinions as Aristotle in some places doth wisely censure, when he saith THESE ARE THE OPINIONS OF PERSONS THAT HAVE RESPECT BUT TO A FEW THINGS. So then we see that this note leadeth us to an administration of knowledge in some such order and policy as the king of Spain in regard of his great dominions useth in state; who though he hath particular councils for several countries and affairs, yet hath one council of State or last resort, that receiveth the advertisements and certificates from all the rest. Hitherto of the diversion, succession, and conference of wits.

CAP. 9.

That The End And Scope Of Knowledge Hath Been Generally Mistaken, And That Men Were Never Well Advised What It Was They Sought; Being The 9th Chapter, Whereof A Fragment (Which Is The End Of The Same Chapter) Is Before.

It appeareth then how rarely the wits and labours of men have been converted to the severe and original inquisition of knowledge; and in those who have pretended, what hurt hath been done by the affectation of professors and the distraction of such as were no professors; and how there was never in effect any conjunction or combination of wits in the first and inducing search, but that every man wrought apart, and would either have his own way or else would go no further than his guide, having in the one case the honour of a first, and in the other the ease of a second; and lastly how in the descent and continuance of wits and labours the succession hath been in the most popular and weak opinions, like unto the weakest natures which many times have most children, and in them also the condition of succession hath been rather to defend and to adorn than to add; and if to add, yet that addition to be rather a refining of a part than an increase of the whole. But the impediments of time and accidents, though they have wrought a general indisposition, yet are they not so peremptory and binding as the internal impediments and clouds in the mind and spirit of man, whereof it now followeth to speak.

The Scripture speaking of the worst sort of error saith, ERRARE FECIT COS IN INVIO ET NON IN VIA. For a man may wander in the way, by rounding up and down. But if men have failed in their very direction and address that error will never by good fortune correct itself. Now it hath fared with men in their contemplations as Seneca saith it fareth with them in their actions, DE PARTIBUS VITAE QUISQUE DELIBERAT, DE SUMMA NEMO. A course very ordinary with men who receive for the most part their final ends from the inclination of their nature, or from common example and opinion, never questioning or examining them, nor reducing them to any clear certainty; and use only to call themselves to account and deliberation touching the means and second ends, and thereby set themselves in the right way to the wrong place. So likewise upon the natural curiosity and desire to know, they have put themselves in way without foresight or consideration of their journey's end.

For I find that even those that have sought knowledge for itself, and not for benefit or ostentation or any practical enablement in the course of their life, have nevertheless propounded to themselves a wrong mark, namely satisfaction (which men call truth) and not operation. For as in the courts and services of princes and states it is a much easier matter to give satisfaction than to do the business; so in the inquiring of causes and reasons it is much easier to find out such causes as will satisfy the mind of man and quiet objections, than such causes as will direct him and give him light to new experiences and inventions. And this did Celsus note wisely and truly, how that the causes which are in use and whereof the knowledges now received do consist, were in time minors and subsequents to the knowledge of the particulars out of which they were induced and collected; and that it was not the light of those causes which discovered particulars, but only the particulars being first found, men did fall on glossing and discoursing of the causes; which is the reason why the learning that now is hath the curse of barrenness, and is courtesanlike, for pleasure, and not for fruit. Nay to compare it rightly, the strange fiction of the poets of the transformation of Scylla seemeth to be a lively emblem of this philosophy and knowledge; a fair woman upwards in the parts of show, but when you come to the parts of use and generation, Barking Monsters; for no better are the endless distorted questions, which ever have been, and of necessity must be, the end and womb of such knowledge.

But yet nevertheless here I may be mistaken, by reason of some which have much in their pen the referring sciences to action and the use of man, which mean quite another matter than I do. For they mean a contriving of directions and precepts for readiness of practice, which I discommend not, so it be not occasion that some quantity of the science be lost; for else it will be such a piece of husbandry as to put away a manor lying somewhat scattered, to buy in a close that lieth handsomely about a dwelling. But my intention contrariwise is to increase and multiply the revenues and possessions of man, and not to trim up only or order with conveniency the grounds whereof he is already stated. Wherefore the better to make myself understood that I mean nothing less than words, and directly to demonstrate the point which we are now upon, that is, what is the true end, scope, or office of knowledge, which I have set down to consist not in any plausible, delectable, reverend, or admired discourse, or any satisfactory arguments, but in effecting and working, and in discovery of particulars not revealed before for the better endowment and help of man's life; I have thought good to make as it were a Kalendar or Inventory of the wealth, furniture, or means of man according to his present estate, as far as it is known; which I do not to shew any universality of sense or knowledge, and much less to make a satire of reprehension in respect of wants and errors, but partly because cogitations new had need of some grossness and inculcation to make them perceived; and chiefly to the end that for the time to come (upon the account and state now made and cast up) it may appear what increase this new manner of use and administration of the stock (if it be once planted) shall bring with it hereafter; and for the time present (in case I should be prevented by death to propound and reveal this new light as I purpose) yet I may at the least give some awaking note both of the wants in man's present condition and the nature of the supplies to be wished; though for mine own part neither do I much build upon my present anticipations, neither do I think ourselves yet learned or wise enough to wish reasonably: for as it asks some knowledge to demand a question not impertinent, so it asketh some sense to make a wish not absurd.

CAP. 10.

The Inventory, Or An Enumeration And View Of Inventions Already Discovered And In Use, Together With A Note Of The Wants And The Nature Of The Supplies, Being The 10th Chapter; And This A Small Fragment Thereof, Being The Preface To The Inventory.

The plainest method and most directly pertinent to this intention, will be to make distribution of sciences, arts, inventions, works, and their portions, according to the use and tribute which they yield and render to the conditions of man's life, and under those several uses, being as several offices of provisions, to charge and tax what may be reasonably exacted or demanded; not guiding ourselves neither by the poverty of experiences and probations, nor according to the vanity of credulous imaginations; and then upon those charges and taxations to distinguish and present, as it were in several columns, what is extant and already found, and what is defective and further to be provided. Of which provisions, because in many of them after the manner of slothful and faulty officers and accomptants it will be returned (by way of excuse) that no such are to be had, it will be fit to give some light of the nature of the supplies, whereby it will evidently appear that they are to be compassed and procured. And yet nevertheless on the other side again it will be as fit to check and control the vain and void assignations and gifts whereby certain ignorant, extravagant, and abusing wits have pretended to indue the state of man with wonders, differing as much from truth in nature as Caesar's Commentaries differeth from the acts of King Arthur or Huon of Bourdeaux in story. For it is true that Caesar did greater things than those idle wits had the audacity to feign their supposed worthies to have done; but he did them not in that monstrous and fabulous manner.

CAP. 11.

The Chapter Immediately Following The Inventory; Being The 11th In Order; A Part Thereof.

It appeareth then what is now in proposition not by general circumlocution but by particular note. No former philosophy varied in terms or method; no new PLACET or speculation upon particulars already known; no referring to action by any manual of practice; but the revealing and discovering of new inventions and operations. This to be done without the errors and conjectures of art, or the length or difficulties of experience; the nature and kinds of which inventions have been described as they could be discovered; for your eye cannot pass one kenning without further sailing; only we have stood upon the best advantages of the notions received, as upon a mount, to shew the knowledges adjacent and confining. If therefore the true end of knowledge not propounded hath bred large error, the best and perfectest condition of the same end not perceived will cause some declination. For when the butt is set up men need not rove, but except the white be placed men cannot level. This perfection we mean not in the worth of the effect, but in the nature of the direction; for our purpose is not to stir up men's hopes, but to guide their travels. The fullness of direction to work and produce any effect consisteth in two conditions, certainty and liberty. Certainty is when the direction is not only true for the most part, but infallible. Liberty is when the direction is not restrained to some definite means, but comprehendeth all the means and ways possible; for the poet saith well SAPIENTIBUS UNDIQUE LATAE SUNT VIAE, and where there is the greatest plurality of change, there is the greatest singularity of choice. Besides as a conjectural direction maketh a casual effect, so a particular and restrained direction is no less casual than an uncertain. For those particular means whereunto it is tied may be out of your power or may be accompanied with an overvalue of prejudice; and so if for want of certainty in direction you are frustrated in success, for want of variety in direction you are stopped in attempt. If therefore your direction be certain, it must refer you and point you to somewhat which, if it be present, the effect you seek will of necessity follow, else may you perform and not obtain. If it be free, then must it refer you to somewhat which if it be absent the effect you seek will of necessity withdraw, else may you have power and not attempt. This notion Aristotle had in light, though not in use. For the two commended rules by him set down, whereby the axioms of sciences are precepted to be made convertible, and which the latter men have not without elegancy surnamed the one the rule of truth because it preventeth deceit, the other the rule of prudence because it freeth election, are the same thing in speculation and affirmation which we now observe. An example will make my meaning attained, and yet percase make it thought that they attained it not. Let the effect to be produced be Whiteness; let the first direction be that if air and water be intermingled or broken in small portions together, whiteness will ensue, as in snow, in the breaking of the waves of the sea and rivers, and the like. This direction is certain, but very particular and restrained, being tied but to air and water. Let the second direction be, that if air be mingled as before with any transparent body, such nevertheless as is uncoloured and more grossly transparent than air itself, that then etc. as glass or crystal, being beaten to fine powder, by the interposition of the air becometh white; the white of an egg being clear of itself, receiving air by agitation becometh white, receiving air by concoction becometh white; here you are freed from water, and advanced to a clear body, and still tied to air. Let the third direction exclude or remove the restraint of an uncoloured body, as in amber, sapphires, etc. which beaten to fine powder become white; in wine and beer, which brought to froth become white. Let the fourth direction exclude the restraint of a body more grossly transparent than air, as in flame, being a body compounded between air and a finer substance than air; which flame if it were not for the smoke, which is the third substance that incorporateth itself and dyeth the flame, would be more perfect white. In all these four directions air still beareth a part. Let the fifth direction then be, that if any bodies, both transparent but in an unequal degree, be mingled as before, whiteness will follow; as oil and water beaten to an ointment, though by settling the air which gathereth in the agitation be evaporate, yet remaineth white; and the powder of glass or crystal put into water, whereby the air giveth place, yet remaineth white, though not so perfect. Now are you freed from air, but still you are tied to transparent bodies. To ascend further by scale I do forbear, partly because it would draw on the example to an over-great length, but chiefly because it would open that which in this work I determine to reserve; for to pass through the whole history and observation of colours and objects visible were too long a digression; and our purpose is now to give an example of a free direction, thereby to distinguish and describe it; and not to set down a form of interpretation how to recover and attain it. But as we intend not now to reveal, so we are circumspect not to mislead; and therefore (this warning being given) returning to our purpose in hand, we admit the sixth direction to be, that all bodies or parts of bodies which are unequal equally, that is in a simple proportion, do represent whiteness; we will explain this, though we induce it not. It is then to be understood, that absolute equality produceth transparence, inequality in simple order or proportion produceth whiteness, inequality in compound or respective order or proportion produceth all other colours, and absolute or orderless inequality produceth blackness; which diversity, if so gross a demonstration be needful, may be signified by four tables; a blank, a chequer, a fret, and a medley; whereof the fret is evident to admit great variety. Out of this assertion are satisfied a multitude of effects and observations, as that whiteness and blackness are most incompatible with transparence; that whiteness keepeth light, and blackness stoppeth light, but neither passeth it; that whiteness or blackness are never produced in rainbows, diamonds, crystals, and the like; that white giveth no dye, and black hardly taketh dye; that whiteness seemeth to have an affinity with dryness, and blackness with moisture; that adustion causeth blackness, and calcination whiteness; that flowers are generally of fresh colours, and rarely black, etc. All which I do now mention confusedly by way of derivation and not by way of induction. This sixth direction, which I have thus explained, is of good and competent liberty for whiteness fixed and inherent, but not for whiteness fantastical or appearing, as shall be afterwards touched. But first do you need a reduction back to certainty or verity; for it is not all position or contexture of unequal bodies that will produce colour; for AQUA FORTIS, oil of VITRIOL, etc. more manifestly, and many other substances more obscurely, do consist of very unequal parts, which yet are transparent and clear. Therefore the reduction must be, that the bodies or parts of bodies so intermingled as before be of a certain grossness or magnitude; for the unequalities which move the sight must have a further dimension and quantity than those which operate many other effects. Some few grains of saffron will give a tincture to a tun of water; but so many grains of civet will give a perfume to a whole chamber of air. And therefore when Democritus (from whom Epicurus did borrow it) held that the position of the solid portions was the cause of colours, yet in the very truth of his assertion he should have added, that the portions are required to be of some magnitude. And this is one cause why colours have little inwardness and necessitude with the nature and proprieties of things, those things resembling in colour which otherwise differ most, as salt and sugar, and contrariwise differing in colour which otherwise resemble most, as the white and blue violets, and the several veins of one agate or marble, by reason that other virtues consist in more subtile proportions than colours do; and yet are there virtues and natures which require a grosser magnitude than colours, as well as scents and divers other require a more subtile; for as the portion of a body will give forth scent which is too small to be seen, so the portion of a body will shew colours which is too small to be endued with weight; and therefore one of the prophets with great elegancy describing how all creatures carry no proportion towards God the creator, saith, THAT ALL THE NATIONS IN RESPECT OF HIM ARE LIKE THE DUST UPON THE BALANCE, which is a thing appeareth but weigheth not. But to return, there resteth a further freeing of this sixth direction; for the clearness of a river or stream sheweth white at a distance, and crystalline glasses deliver the face or any other object falsified in whiteness, and long beholding the snow to a weak eye giveth an impression of azure rather than of whiteness. So as for whiteness in apparition only and representation by the qualifying of the light, altering the INTERMEDIUM, or affecting the eye itself, it reacheth not. But you must free your direction to the producing of such an incidence, impression, or operation, as may cause a precise and determinate passion of the eye; a matter which is much more easy to induce than that which we have passed through; but yet because it hath a full coherence both with that act of radiation (which hath hitherto been conceived and termed so unproperly and untruly by some an effluxion of spiritual species and by others an investing of the INTERMEDIUM with a motion which successively is conveyed to the eye) and with the act of sense, wherein I should likewise open that which I think good to withdraw, I will omit. Neither do I contend but that this motion which I call the freeing of a direction, in the received philosophies (as far as a swimming anticipation could take hold) might be perceived and discerned; being not much other matter than that which they did not only aim at in the two rules of AXIOMS before remembered, but more nearly also in that which they term the form or formal cause, or that which they call the true difference; both which nevertheless it seemeth they propound rather as impossibilities and wishes than as things within the compass of human comprehension. For Plato casteth his burden and saith THAT HE WILL REVERE HIM AS A GOD, THAT CAN TRULY DIVIDE AND DEFINE; which cannot be but by true forms and differences. Wherein I join hands with him, confessing as much as yet assuming to myself little; for if any man call by the strength of his ANTICIPATIONS find out forms, I will magnify him with the foremost. But as any of them would say that if divers things which many men know by instruction and observation another knew by revelation and without those means, they would take him for somewhat supernatural and divine; so I do acknowledge that if any man can by anticipations reach to that which a weak and inferior wit may attain to by interpretation, he cannot receive too high a title. Nay I for my part do indeed admire to see how far some of them have proceeded by their ANTICIPATIONS; but how? It is as I wonder at some blind men, to see what shift they make without their eye-sight; thinking with myself that if I were blind I could hardly do it. Again Aristotle's school confesseth that there is no true knowledge but by causes, no true cause but the form, no true form known except one, which they are pleased to allow; and therefore thus far their evidence standeth with us, that both hitherto there hath been nothing but a shadow of knowledge, and that we propound now that which is agreed to be worthiest to be sought, and hardest to be found. There wanteth now a part very necessary, not by way of supply but by way of caution; for as it is seen for the most part that the outward tokens and badges of excellency and perfection are more incident to things merely counterfeit than to that which is true, but for a meaner and baser sort; as a dubline is more like a perfect ruby than a spinel, and a counterfeit angel is made more like a true angel than if it were an angel coined of China gold; in like manner the direction carrieth a resemblance of a true direction in verity and liberty which indeed is no direction at all. For though your direction seem to be certain and free by pointing you to a nature that is unseparable from the nature you inquire upon, yet if it do not carry you on a degree or remove nearer to action, operation, or light to make or produce, it is but superficial and counterfeit. Wherefore to secure and warrant what is a true direction, though that general note I have given be perspicuous in itself (for a man shall soon cast with himself whether he be ever the nearer to effect and operate or no, or whether he have won but an abstract or varied notion) yet for better instruction I will deliver three particular notes of caution. The first is that the nature discovered be more original than the nature supposed, and not more secondary or of the like degree; as to make a stone bright or to make it smooth it is a good direction to say, make it even; but to make a stone even it is no good direction to say, make it bright or make it smooth; for the rule is that the disposition of any thing referring to the state of it in itself or the parts, is more original than that which is relative or transitive towards another thing. So evenness is the disposition of the stone in itself, but smooth is to the hand and bright to the eye, and yet nevertheless they all cluster and concur; and yet the direction is more unperfect, if it do appoint you to such a relative as is in the same kind and not in a diverse. For in the direction to produce brightness by smoothness, although properly it win no degree, and will never teach you any new particulars before unknown; yet by way of suggestion or bringing to mind it may draw your consideration to some particulars known but not remembered; as you shall sooner remember some practical means of making smoothness, than if you had fixed your consideration only upon brightness by making reflexion, as thus, make it such as you may see your face in it, this is merely secondary, and helpeth neither by way of informing nor by way of suggestion. So if in the inquiry of whiteness you were directed to make such a colour as should be seen furthest in a dark light; here you are advanced nothing at all. For these kinds of natures are but proprieties, effects, circumstances, concurrences, or what else you shall like to call them, and not radical and formative natures towards the nature supposed. The second caution is that the nature inquired be collected by division before composition, or to speak more properly, by composition subaltern before you ascend to composition absolute, etc.

Of The Internal And Profound Errors And Superstitions In The Nature Of The Mind, And Of The Four Sorts Of Idols Or Fictions Which Offer Themselves To The Understanding In The Inquisition Of Knowledge; Being The 16th Chapter, And This A Small Fragment Thereof, Being A Preface To The Inward Elenches Of The Mind.

The opinion of Epicurus that the gods were of human shape, was rather justly derided than seriously confuted by the other sects, demanding whether every kind of sensible creatures did not think their own figure fairest, as the horse, the bull, and the like, which found no beauty but in their own forms, as in appetite of lust appeared. And the heresy of the Anthropomorphites was ever censured for a gross conceit bred in the obscure cells of solitary monks that never looked abroad. Again the fable so well known of QUIS PINXIT LEONEM, doth set forth well that there is an error of pride and partiality, as well as of custom and familiarity. The reflexion also from glasses so usually resembled to the imagery of the mind, every man knoweth to receive error and variety both in colour, magnitude, and shape, according to the quality of the glass. But yet no use hath been made of these and many the like observations, to move men to search out and upon search to give true cautions of the native and inherent errors in the mind of man which have coloured and corrupted all his notions and impressions.

I do find therefore in this enchanted glass four Idols or false appearances of several and distinct sorts, every sort comprehending many subdivisions: the first sort, I call idols of the NATION or TRIBE; the second, idols of the PALACE; the third, idols of the CAVE; and the fourth, idols of the THEATRE, etc.

Here Followeth An Abridgment Of Divers Chapters Of The First Book Of Interpretation Of Nature.

CAP. 12.

That in deciding and determining of the truth of knowledge, men have put themselves upon trials not competent. That antiquity and authority; common and confessed notions; the natural and yielding consent of the mind; the harmony and coherence of a knowledge in itself; the establishing of principles with the touch and reduction of other propositions unto them; inductions without instances contradictory; and the report of the senses; are none of them absolute and infallible evidence of truth, and bring no security sufficient for effects and operations. That the discovery of new works and active directions not known before, is the only trial to be accepted of; and yet not that neither, in ease where one particular giveth light to another; but where particulars induce an axiom or observation, which axiom found out discovereth and designeth new particulars. That the nature of this trial is not only upon the point, whether the knowledge be profitable or no, but even upon the point whether the knowledge be true or no; not because you may always conclude that the Axiom which discovereth new instances is true, but contrariwise you may safely conclude that if it discover not any new instance it is in vain and untrue. That by new instances are not always to be understood new recipes but new assignations, and of the diversity between these two. That the subtilty of words, arguments, notions, yea of the senses themselves, is but rude and gross in comparison of the subtilty of things; and of the slothful and flattering opinions of those which pretend to honour the mind of man in withdrawing and abstracting it from particulars, and of the inducements and motives whereupon such opinions have been conceived and received.

CAP. 13.

Of the error in propounding chiefly the search of causes and productions of things concrete, which are infinite and transitory, and not of abstract natures, which are few and permanent. That these natures are as the alphabet or simple letters, whereof the variety of things consisteth; or as the colours mingled in the painter's shell, wherewith he is able to make infinite variety of faces or shapes. An enumeration of them according to popular note. That at the first one would conceive that in the schools by natural philosophy were meant the knowledge of the efficients of things concrete; and by metaphysic the knowledge of the forms of natures simple; which is a good and fit division of knowledge: but upon examination there is no such matter by them intended. That the little inquiry into the production of simple natures sheweth well that works were not sought; because by the former knowledge some small and superficial deflexions from the ordinary generations and productions may be found out, but the discovery of all profound and radical alteration must arise out of the latter knowledge.

CAP. 14.

Of the error in propounding the search of the materials or dead beginnings or principles of things, and not the nature of motions, inclinations, and applications. That the whole scope of the former search is impertinent and vain;

both because there are no such beginnings, and if there were they could not be known. That the latter manner of search (which is all) they pass over compendiously and slightly as a by-matter. That the several conceits in that kind, as that the lively and moving beginnings of things should be shift or appetite of matter to privation; the spirit of the world working in matter according to platform; the proceeding or fructifying of distinct kinds according to their proprieties; the intercourse of the elements by mediation of their common qualities; the appetite of like portions to unite themselves; amity and discord, or sympathy and antipathy; motion to the centre, with motion of stripe or press; the casual agitation, aggregation, and essays of the solid portions in the void space; motion of shuttings and openings; are all mere nugations; and that the calculating and ordination of the true degrees, moments, limits, and laws of motions and alterations (by means whereof all works and effects are produced), is a matter of a far other nature than to consist in such easy and wild generalities.

CAP. 15.

Of the great error of inquiring knowledge in Anticipations. That I call Anticipations the voluntary collections that the mind maketh of knowledge; which is every man's reason. That though this be a solemn thing, and serves the turn to negotiate between man and man (because of the conformity and participation of men's minds in the like errors), yet towards inquiry of the truth of things and works it is of no value. That civil respects are a lett that this pretended reason should not be so contemptibly spoken of as were fit and medicinable, in regard that hath been too much exalted and glorified, to the infinite detriment of man's estate. Of the nature of words and their facility and aptness to cover and grace the defects of Anticipations. That it is no marvel if these Anticipations have brought forth such diversity and repugnance in opinions, theories, or philosophies, as so many fables of several arguments. That had not the nature of civil customs and government been in most times somewhat adverse to such innovations, though contemplative, there might have been and would have been many more. That the second school of the Academics and the sect of Pyrrho, or the considerers that denied comprehension, as to the disabling of man's knowledge (entertained in Anticipations) is well to be allowed, but that they ought when they had overthrown and purged the floor of the ruins to have sought to build better in place. And more especially that they did unjustly and prejudicially to charge the deceit upon the report of the senses, which admitteth very sparing remedy; being indeed to have been charged upon the Anticipations of the mind, which admitteth a perfect remedy. That the information of the senses is sufficient, not because they err not, but because the use of the sense in discovering of knowledge is for the most part not immediate. So that it is the work, effect, or instance, that trieth the Axiom, and the sense doth but try the work done or not done, being or not being. That the mind of man in collecting knowledge needeth great variety of helps, as well as the hand of man in manual and mechanical practices needeth great variety of instruments. And that it were a poor work that if instruments were removed men would overcome with their naked hands. And of the distinct points of want and insufficiency in the mind of man.

CAP. 16.

That the mind of a man, as it is not a vessel of that content or receipt to comprehend knowledge without helps and supplies, so again it is not sincere, but of an ill and corrupt tincture. Of the inherent and profound errors and superstitions in the nature of the mind, and of the four sorts of Idols or false appearances that offer themselves to the understanding in the inquisition of knowledge; that is to say, the Idols of the Tribe, the Idols of the Palace, the Idols of the Cave, and the Idols of the Theatre. That these four, added to the incapacity of the mind and the vanity and malignity of the affections, leave nothing but impotency and confusion. A recital of the particular kinds of these four Idols, with some chosen examples of the opinions they have begot, such of them as have supplanted the state of knowledge most.

CAP. 17.

Of the errors of such as have descended and applied themselves to experience, and attempted to induce knowledge upon particulars. That they have not had the resolution and strength of mind to free themselves wholly from Anticipations, but have made a confusion and intermixture of Anticipations and observations, and so vanished. That if any have had the strength of mind generally to purge away and discharge all Anticipations, they have not had that greater and double strength and patience of mind, as well to repel new Anticipations after the view and search of particulars, as to reject old which were in their mind before; but have from particulars and history flown up to principles without the mean degrees, and so framed all the middle generalities or axioms, not by way of scale or ascension from particulars, but by way of derivation from principles; whence hath issued the infinite chaos of shadows and notions, wherewith both books and minds have been hitherto, and may be yet hereafter much more pestered. That in the course of those derivations, to make them yet the more unprofitable, they have used when any light of new instance opposite to any assertion appeared, rather to reconcile the instance than to amend the rule. That if any have had or shall have the power and resolution to fortify and inclose his mind against all Anticipations, yet if he have not been or shall not be cautioned by the full understanding of the nature of the mind and spirit of man, and therein of the seats, pores and passages both of knowledge and error, he hath not been nor shall not be possibly able to guide or keep on his course aright. That those that have been conversant in experience and observation have used, when they have intended to discover the cause of any effect, to fix their consideration narrowly and exactly upon that effect itself with all the circumstances thereof, and to vary the trial thereof as many ways as can be devised; which course amounteth but to a tedious curiosity, and ever breaketh off in wondering and not in knowing; and that they have not used to enlarge their observation to match and sort that effect with instances of a diverse subject, which must of necessity be before any cause be found out. That they have passed over the observation of instances vulgar and ignoble, and stayed their attention chiefly upon instances of mark; whereas the other sort are for the most part more significant and of better height and information. That every particular that worketh any effect is a thing compounded (more or less) of diverse single natures, (more manifest and more obscure,) and that it appeareth not to whether of the natures the effect is to be ascribed, and yet notwithstanding they have taken a course without breaking particulars and reducing them by exclusions and inclusions to a definite point, to conclude upon inductions in gross, which empirical course is no less vain than the scholastical. That all such as have sought action and work out of their inquiry have been hasty and pressing to discover some practices for present use, and not to discover Axioms, joining with them the new assignations as their sureties. That the forerunning of the mind to frame recipes upon Axioms at the entrance, is like Atalanta's golden ball that hindereth and interrupteth the course, and is to be inhibited till you have ascended to a certain stage and degree of generalities; which forbearance will be liberally recompensed in the end; and that chance discovereth new inventions by one and one, but science by knots and clusters. That they have not collected sufficient quantity of particulars, nor them in sufficient certainty and subtilty, nor of all several kinds, nor with those advantages and discretions in the entry and sorting which are requisite; and of the weak manner of collecting natural history which hath been used. Lastly that they had no knowledge of the formulary of interpretation, the work whereof is to abridge experience and to make things as certainly found out by Axiom in short time, as by infinite experiences in ages.

CAP. 18.

That the cautels and devices put in practice in the delivery of knowledge for the covering and palliating of ignorance, and the gracing and overvaluing of that they utter, are without number; but none more bold and more hurtful than two; the one that men have used of a few observations upon any subject to make a solemn and formal art, by filling it up with discourse, accommodating it with some circumstances and directions to practice, and digesting it into method, whereby men grow satisfied and secure, as if no more inquiry were to be made of that matter; the other, that men have used to discharge ignorance with credit, in defining all those effects which they cannot attain unto to be out of the compass of art and human endeavour. That the very styles and forms of utterance are so many characters of imposture, some choosing a style of pugnacity and contention, some of satire and reprehension, some of plausible and tempting similitudes and examples, some of great words and high discourse, some of short and dark sentences, some of exactness of method, all of positive affirmation, without disclosing the true motives and proofs of their opinions, or free confessing their ignorance or doubts, except it be now and then for a grace, and in cunning to win the more credit in the rest, and not in good faith. That although men be free from these errors and incumbrances in the will and affection, yet it is not a thing so easy as is conceived to convey the conceit of one man's mind into the mind of another without loss or mistaking, specially in notions new and differing from those that are received. That never any knowledge was delivered in the same order it was invented, no not in the mathematic, though it should seem otherwise in regard that the propositions placed last do use the propositions or grants placed first for their proof and demonstration. That there are forms and methods of tradition wholly distinct and differing, according to their ends whereto they are directed. That there are two ends of tradition of knowledge, the one to teach and instruct for use and practice, the other to impart or intimate for re-examination and progression. That the former of these ends requireth a method not the same whereby it was invented and induced, but such as is most compendious and ready whereby it may be used and applied. That the latter of the ends, which is where a knowledge is delivered to be continued and spun on by a succession of labours, requireth a method whereby it may be transposed to another in the same manner as it was collected, to the end it may be discerned both where the work is weak, and where it breaketh off. That this latter method is not only unfit for the former end, but also impossible for all knowledge gathered and insinuated by Anticipations, because the mind working inwardly of itself, no man can give a just account how he came to that knowledge which he hath received, and that therefore this method is peculiar for knowledge gathered by interpretation. That the discretion anciently observed, though by the precedent of many vain persons and deceivers disgraced, of publishing part, and reserving part to a private succession, and of publishing in a manner whereby it shall not be to the capacity nor taste of all, but shall as it were single and adopt his reader, is not to be laid aside, both for the avoiding of abuse in the excluded, and the stregthening of affection in the admitted. That there are other virtues of tradition, as that there be no occasion given to error, and that it carry a vigour to root and spread against the vanity of wits and injuries of time; all which if they were ever due to any knowledge delivered, or if they were never due to any human knowledge heretofore delivered, yet are now due to the knowledge propounded.

CAP. 19.

Of the impediments which have been in the affections, the principle whereof hath been despair or diffidence, and the strong apprehension of the difficulty, obscurity, and infiniteness which belongeth to the invention of knowledge, and that men have not known their own strength, and that the supposed difficulties and vastness of the work is rather in shew and muster than in state or substance where the true way is taken. That this diffidence hath moved and caused some never to enter into search, and others when they have been entered either to give over or to seek a more compendious course than can stand with the nature of true search. That of those that have refused and prejudged inquiry, the more sober and grave sort of wits have depended upon authors and traditions, and the more vain and credulous resorted to revelation and intelligence with spirits and higher natures. That of those that have entered into search, some having fallen upon some conceits which they after consider to be the same which they have found in former authors, have suddenly taken a persuasion that a man shall but with much labour incur and light upon the same inventions which he might with ease receive from others; and that it is but a vanity and self-pleasing of the wit to go about again, as one that would rather have a flower of his own gathering, than much better gathered to his hand. That the same humour of sloth and diffidence suggesteth that a man shall but revive some ancient opinion, which was long ago propounded, examined, and rejected. And that it is easy to err in conceit that a man's observation or notion is the same with a former opinion, both because new conceits must of necessity be uttered in old words, and because upon true and erroneous grounds men may meet in consequence or conclusion, as several lines or circles that cut in some one point. That the greatest part of those that have descended into search have chosen for the most artificial and compendious course to induce principles out of particulars, and to reduce all other propositions unto principles; and so instead of the nearest way, have been led to no way or a mere labyrinth. That the two contemplative ways have some resemblance with the old parable of the two moral ways, the one beginning with incertainty and difficulty, and ending in plainness and certainty, and the other beginning with shew of plainness and certainty, and ending in difficulty and incertainty. Of the great and manifest error and untrue conceit or estimation of the infiniteness of particulars, whereas indeed all prolixity is in discourse and derivations; and of the infinite and most laborious expense of wit that hath been employed upon toys and matters of no fruit or value. That although the period of one age cannot advance men to the furthest point of interpretation of nature, (except the work should be undertaken with greater helps than can be expected), yet it cannot fail in much less space of time to make return of many singular commodities towards the state and occasions of man's life. That there is less reason of distrust in the course of interpretation now propounded than in any knowledge formerly delivered, because this course doth in sort equal men's wits, and leaveth no great advantage or preeminence to the perfect and excellent motions of the spirit. That to draw a straight line or to make a circle perfect round by aim of hand only, there must be a great difference between an unsteady and unpractised hand and a steady and practised, but to do it by rule or compass it is much alike.

CAP. 21.
Of the impediments which have been in the two extreme humours of admiration of antiquity and love of novelty, and again of over-servile reverence or over-light scorn of the opinions of others.

CAP. 22.
Of the impediments which have been in the affection of pride, specially of one kind, which is the disdain of dwelling and being conversant much in experiences and particulars, specially such as are vulgar in occurrency, and base and ignoble in use. That besides certain higher mysteries of pride, generalities seem to have a

dignity and solemnity, in that they do not put men in mind of their familiar actions, in that they have less affinity with arts mechanical and illiberal, in that they are not so subject to be controlled by persons of mean observation, in that they seem to teach men that they know not, and not to refer them to that they know. All which conditions directly feeding the humour of pride, particulars do want. That the majesty of generalities, and the divine nature of the mind in taking them (if they be truly collected, and be indeed the direct reflexions of things,) cannot be too much magnified. And that it is true that interpretation is the very natural and direct intention, action, and progression of the understanding delivered from impediments. And that all Anticipation is but a deflexion or declination by accident.

CAP. 25.
Of the impediments which have been in the state of heathen religion and other superstitions and errors of religion. And that in the true religion there hath not nor is any impediment, except it be by accident or intermixture of humour. That a religion which consisteth in rites and forms of adoration, and not in confessions and beliefs, is adverse to knowledge; because men having liberty to inquire and discourse of Theology at pleasure, it cometh to pass that all inquisition of nature endeth and limiteth itself in such metaphysical or theological discourse; whereas if men's wits be shut out of that port, it turneth them again to discover, and so to seek reason of reason more deeply. And that such was the religion of the Heathen. That a religion that is jealous of the variety of learning, discourse, opinions, and sects, (as misdoubting it may shake the foundations,) or that cherisheth devotion upon simplicity and ignorance, as ascribing ordinary effects to the immediate working of God, is adverse to knowledge. That such is the religion of the Turk, and such hath been the abuse of Christian religion at some several times, and in some several factions. And of the singular advantage which the Christian religion hath towards the furtherance of true knowledge, in that it excludeth and interdicteth human reason, whether by interpretation or anticipation, from examining or discussing of the mysteries and principles of faith.

CAP. 26.
Of the impediments which have been in the nature of society and the policies of state. That there is no composition of estate or society, nor order or quality of persons, which have not some point of contrariety towards true knowledge. That monarchies incline wits to profit and pleasure, and commonwealths to glory and vanity. That universities incline wits to sophistry and affectation, cloisters to fables and unprofitable subtilty, study at large to variety; and that it is hard to say, whether mixture of contemplations with an active life, or retiring wholly to contemplations, do disable and hinder the mind more.

(Back Cover.)
Philosophy.
Line 1: see commentary

Line 2: libri dimidium est, pagina 34

Line 3: pagellarum numeri veri

Writing on the Back Cover of VALERIUS TERMINUS

The writing in the original is on the outside of the last leaf, which is in fact the cover. The front cover, if there ever was one, is lost. The ink with which the line containing the symbols is written corresponds with that in the body of the manuscript; and the line itself is placed symmetrically in the middle of the page, near the top. The two lower lines are apparently by another hand, probably of later date, certainly in ink of a different colour, and paler. The word "Philosophy" is in Bacon's own hand, written lightly in the upper corner at the left, and is no doubt merely a docket inserted afterwards when he was sorting his papers. What connexion there was between the note and the manuscript it is impossible to say. But it is evidently a careful memorandum of something, set down by somebody when the manuscript was at hand; and so many of the characters resemble those adopted to represent the planets and the signs of the zodiac, that one is led to suspect in it a note of the positions of the heavenly bodies at the time of some remarkable accident;—perhaps the plague, of which 30,578 persons died in London, during the year ending 22nd December, 1603. The period of the commencement, the duration, or the cessation of such an epidemic might naturally be so noted.

Now three of the characters clearly represent respectively Mercury, Aquarius, and Sagittarius. The sign for Jupiter, as we find it in old books, is so like a 4, that the first figure of 45 may very well have been meant for it. The monogram at the beginning of the line bears a near resemblance to the sign of Capricorn in its most characteristic feature. And the mark over the sign of Aquarius appears to be an abbreviation of that which usually represents the Sun. (The blot between 1603 and B is nothing; being only meant to represent a figure 6 blotted out with the finger before the ink was dry.) Suspecting therefore that the writing contained a note of the positions of Mercury and Jupiter in the year 1603, I sent a copy to a scientific friend and asked him if from such data he could determine the month indicated. He found upon a rough calculation (taking account of mean motions only) that Jupiter did enter the sign of Sagittarius about the 10th of August, 1603, and continued there for about a twelvemonth; that the Sun entered Aquarius about the 12th or 13th of January, 1603-4; and that Mercury was about the 16th or 17th of the same month in the 26th or 27th degree of Capricorn: —coincidences which would have been almost conclusive as to the date indicated, if Capricorn had only stood where Aquarius does, and vice versa. But their position as they actually stood in the manuscript is a formidable, if not fatal, objection to the interpretation.

According to another opinion with which I have been favoured, the first monogram is a NOTA BENE; the next group may mean DIES MERCURII (Wednesday) 26TH JANUARY, 1603; and the rest refers to something not connected with astronomy. But to this also there is a serious objection. The 26th of January, 1603-4, was a Friday, and it seems to me very improbable that any Englishman would have described the preceding January as belonging to the year 1603. Bacon himself invariably dated according to the civil year, and the occasional use of the historical year in loose memoranda would have involved all his dates in confusion. I should think it more probable that the writer (who may have been copying a kind of notation with which he was not familiar) miscopied the sign of Venus into that of Mercury; in which case it would mean Friday, 26th January, 1603-4. But even then the explanation would he unsatisfactory, as leaving so much unexplained. Those however who are familiar with old manuscripts relating to such subjects may probably be able to interpret the whole.

Lightning Source UK Ltd.
Milton Keynes UK
UKOW01f1452210916

283490UK00002B/423/P